"Evil is . . . a living, spiritual being, perverted and perverting. A terrible reality. Mysterious and frightening."

—Pope Paul VI

DOES THE DEVIL EXIST?

Alan Landsburg, TV's #1 explorer of the unknown, investigates the shocking truth behind today's occult explosion. Evidence that includes:
* Satanic cults in America
* The Hitchhiking Demon
* The human sacrifice to save a king
* Death spells that can't be stopped

They're just a few of the fantastic, fully documented facts that prove the existence of an awesome supernatural force in our ultramodern world . . .

IN SEARCH OF MAGIC AND WITCHCRAFT
by Alan Landsburg

D1379830

ABOUT THE AUTHOR

ALAN LANDSBURG is a successful film and television producer, heading up his own production company in Los Angeles, California. He was instrumental in bringing the von Däniken phenomenon to the attention of the American public through TV by producing "In Search of Ancient Astronauts." Alan Landsburg is also the author of *In Search of Ancient Mysteries* and *The Outer Space Connection*. He is currently working on a weekly television series, "In Search of . . .," which has been on the air since September, 1976. *In Search of Magic and Witchcraft* and five other books on extraterrestrials, monsters, lost civilizations, strange phenomena and people, are based on the series.

In Search of
Magic
and
Witchcraft
by Alan Landsburg

Foreword by Leonard Nimoy

BANTAM BOOKS · TORONTO · NEW YORK · LONDON

DEDICATION

To my friend Howard Lipstone, whose support made it possible for this book to exist, and to Sylvan Covey who has always believed that all dreams are possible.

ACKNOWLEDGMENTS

As one of the producers of the "In Search of . . ." television series, Hans Holzer provided me with a great deal of information and guidance in the presentation of this book.

I wish also to acknowledge the following photographers whose work appears in this book: Andrew Reichline, Linda Otto, Julian Charrington and Hans Holzer.

RLI: $\dfrac{\text{VLM 9 (VLR 8–10)}}{\text{IL 9+}}$

IN SEARCH OF MAGIC AND WITCHCRAFT
A Bantam Book / February 1977

Bantam Books are published by Bantam Books, Inc. Its trademark, consisting of the words "Bantam Books" and the portrayal of a bantam, is registered in the United States Patent Office and in other countries. Marca Registrada, Bantam Books, Inc., 666 Fifth Avenue, New York, New York 10019.

PRINTED IN THE UNITED STATES OF AMERICA

CONTENTS

AUTHOR'S NOTE

The chronicle of discovery amassed in this volume is the work of many people. More than 100 researchers, scientists and skilled filmmakers participated in the various quests. For simplicity's sake we have comingled our experiences into a single first person narrative so that we may share with you the essence and excitement of the hunt without a clutter of personal introductions. As author and chief chronicler of the work we have done, I owe an enormous debt of gratitude to those who joined me in the field to explore the world of mystery. To all of those dedicated workers committed to "In Search of . . ." I say thank you. This book is as much yours as mine.

Alan Landsburg

FOREWORD

My first working association with the television series "In Search of . . ." was a narration session in which I was asked to read aloud the major objectives of the various categories—Lost Civilizations, Unexplained Phenomena, Missing Persons, Magic and Witchcraft, Myths and Monsters, and finally Extraterrestrials. The roll call of subjects was mind-bending. I kept on reading the sentences appended to the list but my mind was focused on the prospect of walking the electrifying path between what is known scientific fact and what is far-out science fiction.

Alan Landsburg is a much honored producer of television documentary films, and his extraordinarily talented staff of directors, writers, cameramen and editors were out in the field collecting some of the most unusual images ever recorded on a television screen. What appealed to me most was the very range of subjects. On the one hand we might be searching for Amelia Earhart lost on a trans-Pacific flight in 1937, on the other for the famed Count Dracula of myth and fact. Who did build Stonehenge? Where did UFOs land? Is there really life after death? Do plants speak? The quest and the questions presented virtually an unlimited source of adventure. More than a hundred people were scattered around the world recording pieces of data, clues, evidence which fulfilled Hamlet's promise that "there are more things on earth than you have dreamed of in your philosophy."

I liked the sense of butting up against old ideas and demonstrating that new explanations were possible. In pursuit of old baffling mysteries, the programs opened new directions to pursue more illuminating answers. For all of these reasons I immersed myself in the fascinating game. It's good to know that our television series "In Search of . . ." has now become something of a byword for many viewers.

This book is a chronicle of the efforts that have gone into making the television series. It's a fascinating logbook to me, filled with the excitement of overcoming the impossible and the fulfillment of discovery. I hope you find it as intriguing as I did.

Leonard Nimoy

INTRODUCTION

When I was a young boy, nature held a certain fascination for me. I felt at peace with the vast sky, a dome around me. There I saw the seasons, the movement of stars and the moon. Through education I was introduced to the facts, literature, and myths of many nations. I learned of the mystery of religion and philosophy, of the mystery of people and power. I worked to establish a professional life.

Then I worked to fulfill myself as a person. Most of my working life has been spent documenting on film the crucial events of my time. It was only in my later professional life that I began to realize that there just might be more than meets my eye about the science of the universe. I was fascinated by my experiences in Egypt. What was the strange, electromagnetic force that was being pumped from the interior of pyramids? I learned in fascinating detail how mummies were preserved. I wondered if immortality could really be attained.

I wanted to find more information on unseen energies and forces and how they work. This might be a Chinese puzzle, but I would like to take you anyway on this journey with me, to see that magic and witchcraft (the use of natural forces) are alive and well.

1
What is Magic?

All early human development was surrounded by a secondary force called magic. What do I mean when I say magic? Today, people relate magic or magicians to vaudeville entertainment. Magic is a trick with a perfectly logical explanation behind it that the viewer does not know but only suspects. Since the gullible are deceived by sleight-of-hand, magic is generally accepted as a phony, artificial, clever game that was designed to relax and entertain. A modern magician can indeed be the greatest of all skeptics when it comes to accepting extrasensory perception or anything transcending the five senses.

After I saw the Amazing Randi perform on television, I went to the library to check on his claim that he could imitate anything a practitioner of true "Magick" could do. I didn't find any proof of that, but I discovered that Randi, a Canadian popular with young audiences all over the world, had written a detailed book accusing psychic Uri Geller of trickery. I suppose that for a prestidigitator to admit there is *something* he can't imitate would be deadly. Milbourne Christopher, another world-famous professional magician, who wrote what some consider the best biography of the late Harry Houdini, also came to grips with the "other" kind of magic—the psychic feats performed by the late medium Arthur Ford. Despite Ford's inability to defend himself against allegations of fraud, being in spiritland himself, there is still *something* that the stage magician cannot and will never be able to do. But the magic I'm talking about is quite different. I'm speaking of magic as it was known to the ancients. To "make magic" even in today's society means *to set forces in motion*. "Good medicine" to the American

Indian was a positive influence. What we might call positive magic was used by the Stone Age people. This use of psychic energy later became "white magic," as opposed to "black magic."

Whether used for constructive or destructive purposes—just as man himself can be both good and bad —there is really no difference among the techniques of magic. Magic is merely a force. It does not differentiate between good and evil. It is the person who knows and uses this force to get certain results who determines the qualitative shading of the process.

Rollo Ahmed, the British researcher described by peer Dennis Wheatley as "a master who has devoted a lifetime to acquiring a first-hand knowledge of that grim 'other world' " points out that the black arts differ from the "white" not in method but in purpose. After all, all magic ritual is but an attempt to extend man's powers beyond the ordinary, beyond the limits imposed on "ordinary" people by education and circumstances. Only the magician knows how to break through this barrier.

Of course, what is magic at one point in history may be considered commonplace at a later date. Certainly anyone able to produce electricity during the early eighteenth century would have been suspected of supernatural powers—because he would have had knowledge of *natural* law which the rest of humanity lacked. Likewise, today's magic practitioner performs feats that are unusual only because humanity does not share his more extensive knowledge of what is possible in nature. The line between religion and magic is so hard to define, whereas science as an experience is clearly defined; an idea accepted through common reason becomes a law. A law is likely to deal with something you can see and *repeat*. But anyone who feels that science organizes all, should remember that today's improbability can be tomorrow's common occurrence.

I was trying to find out whether there are certain elements in magic that will *always* be magical regardless of the accomplishments of empirical science. In particular, these might be areas of influence from variable to variable, mind to mind, instead of mind to machine or another constant. If we were truly at the height of our rapid technical progress, we would now have the robots envisioned by science fiction writer Ray Bradbury. But we have not really made such great progress in understanding the inner workings of the individual. What is mind power and how can it be fully utilized? This question must be answered before we can see what or if there is magic.

A priest or shaman in primitive society was a person with psychic abilities who served as go-between for his people and the deities. They could accept his position if they wished, and those who did benefited from it, of course. Even in those early days there was "establishment." The outsider practicing magic on his own was considered a poor security risk. A Stone Age magician had no love for amateurs. A strong belief in magic made it a potent force, and this force could not be haphazardly dealt with. It worked better when the forces in the minds of the tribe were directed to *one* person among them. Any other practitioner of magic would only split the force and make it less effective; therefore, the "official" magician prospered.

Does *belief* in magic make it work? Belief is similar to prayer in that energy patterns can be shaped or sent out in a particular direction. I recently talked to some friends who think belief in the probability of an unusual feat will help it happen. A person is experiencing something, but actually he isn't. "It's all in your mind" is an expression one hears from time to time. But belief is not so much a positive attitude toward a phenomenon, as a reserve of positive energy a person can store up and draw upon. People hope that prayer works because they pour emotional energy into an idea, not because of key words or phrases they use. The words they use do have special meaning to them, and as with everything, the *specific* is stronger. How intense they are, and what form their prayers take will determine the outcome.

One day I watched an Indian fakir perform the well-known rope trick. I promised myself not to be hypnotized into believing that the rope would rise of its own volition. I wasn't. But this particular magician used

3

physical means to deceive his audience. There was that very thin, *nearly* invisible thread that pulled the rope into an upright position. Yet, all around me in the audience, people gasped and took the performance at face value.

Mundus vult decipi, decipimur is the magicians' professional motto. It means, "The world wants to be fooled, so let us fool it."

How true.

Magic is a volatile thing: it cannot be used to solve everyday problems and matters that a person is able to resolve in other ways. Magic can be the way when *other* methods fail. But can it be the force one can turn to under heavy stress? Does man need a psychologically motivated "out"?

The magic of primitive man differs from that of today's seeker in the degree of sophistication, not in the basic concept, I think. This concept is not to alter or bypass natural laws. The natural laws work strongly and, to our eye, freely. Magic is the application of knowledge, techniques, and skills to natural laws. But first we must realize that laws *exist*, and then with the help of such knowledge utilize them much like we utilize oil or natural gas.

To Benjamin Franklin, the heavy-duty cables that carry electricity today would be magic compared to a key, a string, a bolt of lightning. If he had known that there was a better way to get electric power, he would have used it. Those who are already into practicing magic simply know some of these more-efficient ways to harness the powers of natural laws. They apply their methods quietly, without fanfare. It is held by secret cults that dispensing magic power indiscriminately lessens its effectiveness.

It's human nature to look for a shortcut. Whenever a person strives for the important, the desirable, or the difficult, he tries to eliminate all or most of the obstacles and to make the results perfect in every detail. "Honesty is the best policy," but primitive instincts in man always look for a better, quicker way to the goal.

Because of my previous two books, I have received many letters from people who seek magic as the means

4

to satisfy their desires. So many are only dimly aware of what magic really is and how it works. The very idea of using magic is tantalizing—and monumental—to the mind. "I need a magic potion to get my boyfriend back," a young lady wrote from Milwaukee, offering ten dollars for a successful formula. Another correspondent from New York City noted that "if magic really works, as you hint at, why is it everybody isn't using it? Like the Russians, for instance." I don't know, but I referred the correspondent to Alistair Crowley's teachings: at least she would learn what it is like when magic does work.

I myself asked a certain Hollywood wizard to try to influence one of my clients, if he indeed could do so. I had nothing to lose—if he succeeded, I had sold a show; if he failed, I got my skepticism back. He asked for a photograph of the "subject" (that part was easy) but also some hair (that part was not). In the end, the test wasn't attempted. I got sidetracked and succeeded without it.

The gap between the potency of the word *magic* and the actual accomplishment may be quite wide. The belief that magic can be applied is the first step to working the natural law. Usually, before the process even starts, the mind of the door jumps ahead to the accomplished feat. Because of this state of anticipation, believers in magic are looked upon as dreamers living in an unreal world. But do not confuse this state of happy expectation with some *very real* accomplishments in the field of magic.

History is filled with man's attempts to harness his world and to understand the omnipotent power around him. What seems to make this power greater than the individual?

The majority of mankind is satisfied to let organized religion of one kind or another answer that question for them, and to accept more or less blindly what fate —as ruled by the deity or deities—has in store for them. But there is a minority that, by character or inclination, refuses to accept blindly what they think they can change. They are the seekers of magic, the ones who postulate that there are ways to get around the

5

ordinary order of things, "if you know the secret." Magic is that way. In every civilization, even today, there are "above-ground" religions and "underground" (or secret) cults, side by side, mutually nonexclusive, and occasionally at odds with each other.

Man tends to *worship* what he cannot grasp intellectually.

Religious experience is the process of worshiping a power greater than one's self. Religious expression is that which passes from physical man to a nonphysical deity, a state of mind, a way of life that expresses love for and trust in God. Religion means to "bind back," or to keep a close tie with a deity, but the very word assumes that this tie has *already* been established in the distant past. In falling to one's knees when worshiping a deity, one automatically accepts the fact that the deity was there first. Worshiping is a tradition and thus reaffirms ties established sometime in the past.

Let us explore the ties we have to the powerful "supernatural" forces. Most people have a strong sense of destiny. And so far we have no evidence for believing that any species other than man has this psychic awareness. Also, nonhuman forms of life do not appear to recognize the two big doors—one to good and one to evil. Demons and angels are quite incomprehensible to the animal mind. To me, the first clue to the supernatural came when I defined the existence of the soul or the "something" that survives, even though the body goes into the earth or the sea, or, by fire, into the wind. It's amazing that ancient man seems to have given every animate or inanimate thing a consciousness similar to his own.

But suppose magic is believing—is it possible to liberate the divine soul within and acquire supernatural power? Is it possible for a person to exercise authority over the "spirits ruling the world" and compel all nature to submit to the human will? In our never-ceasing quest for self-realization we waver between two paths: the inward self-liberating way, and the outward projection of the personality, which has as its goal absolute mastery over the universe.

Both the magician and the scientist use the second

6

process. They both seek to transform the world by man-made techniques. Old books on alchemy call to mind the modern chemist; as Eliphas Levi, the nineteeth-century seer, declared in *Transcendental Magic:* "Magic is the science of the secrets of nature."

The scientist uses material methods to obtain results, and accepts only that which he can test at will under conditions he controls. The magician, on the other hand, uses the powers of mind and imagination to obtain tangible results. But his system is as well organized and specific as the scientist's—only his values differ. Where the scientist is limited to demonstrated facts for his knowledge, the magician regards ideas, thought forms, verbalizations, etc. as equally tangible and therefore powerful. Religion argues that the magician is seeking to acquire power over nature and wrongly tramples on territorial rights of the priest—and to the church this is heresy.

Primitive people all over the world still use and continue to develop the basic techniques of magic. Many of these people believe that objects react upon one another by a kind of sympathy or affinity, the rules of which were defined by Sir James Frazier (1854–1941) in his famous work *The Golden Bough:* "Things that have once been in contact with each other continue to act upon one another at a distance after the physical contact has been severed": and, furthermore, "Like produces like and an effect resembles its cause." For example, a sorcerer can use a person's nail clipping or a lock of hair to "bewitch" a person from a distance. *Black* magic is the worst form of psychic assault, for its intention is the enslavement of the mind and body of another person.

On one of my trips to London I decided to go to the British Museum, which has probably the world's most complete library of books dealing with demonology and witchcraft. Among other rare and ancient volumes, I marveled at the sixteenth-century editions of the *Lemegaton,* the "Bible" of demonology, in which thousands of demons, both good and evil, are enumerated along with their areas of activity, and of course the spells and incantations that make them come forth

7

and do your bidding! All this is organized like a feudal empire, with higher "princes" and lesser "barons" ruling the universe, including Earth. Maybe these were merely archetypes, symbolic thought forms, but to the medieval magician they were as real as flesh-and-blood people and could actually be contacted.

According to tradition, the person who deals with magic is convinced that powerful spirits or gods rule the four major elements—fire, earth, air, and water. In addition, there are lesser spirits residing in the mountains and rivers, and in the animal world. All of these have no alternative but to obey the commands of the person who has mastered "the magical arts."

I checked with my friend Professor Hans Holzer, who has investigated so many claims of true magic, to discover whether there was anything at all to this sort of incantation. He assured me that going through the ritual of "raising a demon" can be quite terrifying and impressive at the same time.

"But did you actually *see* any demons?" I insisted.

"Well, I *thought* I did," Holzer replied somewhat enigmatically. "Of course you realize that the power of suggestion can be very persuasive under the right stimulation and in an environment that excludes ordinary elements such as light, sound, and 'worldly' intrusions. No matter what I experienced, it was *a kind of magic.*"

Magic was originally aimed toward solving problems that arise in agricultural societies. For example, crop magic to make crops grow better despite lack of rain, despite lack of sunshine, and despite logic.

People feel secure if there is someone in charge who knows how to take care of a problem. In ancient times, people trusted their most precious possession—food— to the care of a higher force. These people prayed to whatever deity they believed was responsible for crops, putting it all into the deity's hands, leaving it to his or her good will or decision whether the crop should be helped. Now, if the deity wasn't willing, man had no choice but to accept that in good faith. But to help along the deity with presumably good faith, the alternate route—magic—could be attempted. Where prayer is total supplication, with the recipient unable to influence the decision in any manner, magic is a process of active participation by the supplicant in the process of making something occur: thus, there is incentive. Of course, there is this difference: anyone can pray, no previous experience is necessary. But not everyone is a good magician. One has to have studied nature's laws and understood their workings before one can apply them to the situation at hand. If the application of magic fails nevertheless, it is not magic that is at fault, but the one applying it—he simply did not know his techniques well enough!

But let's take this one step further. Even today, a ruler will not ignore the expressed thoughts of his subjects, if enough of them unite to express them. This is an indirect influence. To make this influence of thought effective, it must be properly united and directed toward a specific goal. It then becomes a power beam ramming through the desired goal. Cleve Backster, a serious researcher in plant sentience, has shown that his flowers grow better when spoken to and respond to love, as well as to the thought of taking a match and burning a plant's leaf! Energy changes appear on his sensitive recording instruments. The point is, if you set up a positive energy flow toward your plant, it will help it grow. I'm not saying that the "spirit" of the plant is grateful to you for your attitude or anything as outlandish as that. There is nothing personal in the relationship between plant owner and plant, but there is a movement of small particles of energy positively charged with growth instructions that somehow increase the ordinary growth impulse of the plant. This ordinary impulse may be suffering from poor surroundings as plants often do in civilized environments, or lack of air or food or light: the positive energy supplied by the green thumb (through his expressions of love) will give the plant a better chance of surviving.

Johnny Carson's *Tonight* show, before millions of viewers, demonstrated plant response: by today's attitude, we might place this in the category of "magic."

In a similar way, primitive magicians influenced crops to grow. Magic is part of witchcraft ritual (but witchcraft is much more than magic, as I will show in later chapters). The witches of old practicing "sympathetic magic," tried to induce the grain to grow higher by getting astride brooms. I discovered this very sensible explanation for the witchcraft broom ride when I leafed through books on magic and witchcraft, notably Gerald Gardner's *The Meaning of Witchcraft* and Hans Holzer's *The Truth About Witchcraft*. So the witches rode or rather pretended to ride their brooms in a circle around the fields, all the while "talking" to the seeds in the ground—"Please grow nice and tall so we have lots of bread!"

Did it work? Well, if the Backster experiments with plants are any indication, it must have worked at least some of the time. Especially when the witches were really frantic and put their strongest emotional outpourings into the ritual.

In today's society it's hard not to be affected by the word in longhand or print or by the electronic word of mouth, radio, and television. Writing and printing were thousands of years away: in those days, word of mouth was limited to your small circle and those small circles you dealt with. The village adept was the person who realized that certain formulas worked better than others. Belief in verbalization of desires has been innate in man from the very beginning of his existence. Say the right word, and things happen. Say the wrong word, and you're in trouble. This is a child's first and best tool. Words, in the description of California psychiatrist R. Newman, are "triggers to action." Proper verbalization, the right formula, is a must for magic to be effective.

The tighter the wording of the incantation, the more potent the magic is likely to be. Instead of saying, "Please, my little grain stocks, my little bearded friends, won't you try so hard to grow higher no matter how bad the weather is, because we all need the grain of life," primitive man would say, "Grain grow tall." He repeated this often because he believed, just as most of our parents believed, that repetition strengthens effectiveness. Carefully choosing the words was not enough. One had to be careful that the phrases weren't too easily understood by outsiders, because then the magic would lose its potency. So this brought about formulas that were known only to insiders. Eventually, the adepts no longer knew what they meant and kept repeating them without being able to visualize the meaning. "O lord of the trees, descend upon us and bless our children," may mean nothing more than a request to Mother Nature to send a little rain to help the crops.

Reading books on magic and witchcraft can lead to the strangest discoveries: for instance, that the pagans worshiped under tall trees because the power from growing things was used in their rites. Or that churches were originally built to take the place of outdoor sanctuaries—that is why some cathedrals are very roomy, with high ceilings, to give you that outdoor feeling. It was also customary, according to most authorities, such as anthropologist Margaret Murray, to build a Christian church on the exact spot where an old pagan sanctuary had stood. The average Joe might think that was because it replaced the Old Religion and the spot was already familiar to the people living in the region. But that is only part of the reason. The accumulated emotional energies of worshipers, going back centuries, stick to the area and can be utilized by priests to create a stronger religious atmosphere for their mass—the Christian answer to the ancient pagan ritual.

I read where biologist-physician-psychiatrist John Pierrakos discovered that trees have energy fields that can be measured. In a scientific presentation called "The Energy Field in Man and Nature," Dr. Pierrakos, who works at the Institute of Bioenergetic Analysis in New York, shows how the flow of energy in all living things consists of several layers with different purposes, not just one field. The pulsation rate of plants differs greatly from plant to plant. Some trees pulsate twelve to fourteen times a minute, others even more often. But plants pulsate more slowly than do humans and animals.

The best feeling in the world is to wake up filled with positive energy. You may have a sudden thought about

11

calling a friend. This friend gets a flash before the telephone even rings. This is how magic is related to ESP. With positive energy you make things happen. You go through a particular day without fears of failure. People respond to you. You become happy. The bus comes on time. You pass a friend. You are filled with positive energy. Your appointment goes right. You think, I hope he'll buy my suggestion, and as you visualize it silently in your mind, something jumps from yours to his and he's thinking along *your* wavelength. To him this is a heightened moment in life, an original thought that's just sprung up. Remember, magic works best when the one on whom it is being worked does not recognize it as such.

If you want to use magic to obtain a better job, you must attempt it with a relaxed, confident attitude—you already know that your technique will work—you don't doubt it. Of course, you must be sure of what you want, and that you are capable of delivering once you get your position or improvement. If you are sure of your desire and can form a clear thought about it, you're on the road to making it *real*. This is the road to success. The way you stay on this road is to be sure of your desires and be able to express them in a few, direct words that require immediate action. The whole system rests on this immediate action. Wishing doesn't make it so. "I hope he likes me," you say. Be kind to your fellow man and he will like you. So next, think something like, I will impress him with the good quality of my work and I'll be the right person for the position and he will ask me to take it. This is the right approach to "magical" phrasing.

These verbalizations, subtle commands, if you wish, are slipped into the other person's unconscious gently, *not* via concentration. Shaking hands or some kind of physical touch makes you both aware of each other's presence: an additional physical link comparable to the magical idea of having a part of a person's physical self, tact. You must establish contact to be most effective. such as hairs or a photo, as means of establishing con- It also involves psychometry, the art of "reading" a person's past, present, or future from the mere touch of an object the person has had upon his body for some time.

The line between suggestion and magic is not always distinct. Magic of this kind is nothing more than very intense, organized suggestion plus thought transference. Of course all unknown, unseen things were magic to the people of old. Man's constant attempts to change exterior, natural phenomena by applying secret formulas through ritual and ceremony is an essential part of his way of thinking and behaving. I knew that man tried to influence the forces around him from the very earliest times onward, but when did he codify his rituals so that others might copy them and get equal results? During a lull in filming, I went up to the Metropolitan Museum in New York City, where there is an excellent library for the use of scholars working in the field of antiquities. With their help, I discovered that the magic formulas thought to be most effective were committed to writing several thousands of years ago. We can trace the origins of ceremonial magic to the Akkadian-Chaldean inscriptions of Nineveh dating from the second millennium B.C. The thought verbalizations show a highly sophisticated choice of words, which suggest a long tradition of magic practice:

> They are seven! They are seven!
> In the depths of the ocean they are seven!
> In the brilliancy of the heavens they are seven!
> They proceed from the ocean depths, from the hidden retreat. They are neither male nor female, those which stretch themselves out like chains, they have no spouse, they do not produce children; they are strangers to benevolence.

Oddly, prior to the Akkadian texts we have only the evidence of cave paintings and primitive sculpture, which suggest man's eternal preoccupation with magic: crops, success in hunting, the warding off of sickness or misfortune or of evil spirits. Magic was as necessary to everyday life as tending your own garden. Somehow, magic, religion, and even art seemed to be interwoven with one another. As Montague Summers put it, "The

13

reason why man came forth believing in terrors and evils is simply that terrors and evils were there and very real and the simplicity of primitive man was sensibly conscious of their activities and of their presence all about him."

Ancient Nineveh seems to have shared our own confusion between the operations of black magic and white magic. Their religious system appears to have taken both into consideration, but the two elements were so intermingled that they resulted in what Butler, in his book, *Ritual Magic,* termed "an extremely elaborate and well-developed demonology."

> The magician has bewitched me with his magic, he has bewitched me with his magic;
> He who has fashioned images corresponding to my whole appearance has bewitched my whole appearance;
> He has seized the magic draught prepared for me and has soiled my garments;
> He has torn my garments and has mingled his magic herb with the dust of my feet;
> May the fire-God, the hero, turn their magic to naught!

So there it is. We might be in Salem or the New Forest. The two streams of magic are already clearly defined: the simple magic spells and incantations of primitive magic and the highly complex and demanding rituals of ceremonial magic binding angels and demons to do one's bidding.

> The wicked God, the wicked Demon
> The demon of the desert, the demon of the mountain,
> The demon of the sea, the demon of the marsh,
> Spirit of the heavens, conjure it!
> Spirit of the earth, conjure it!

By and by the civil authorities became interested in magical practices. Hammurabi legislated for his community: "If a man has laid a charge of witchcraft on another man and has not justified it, he upon whom the witchcraft charge is laid, shall go to the holy river, and if the holy river overcome him, he who accused him shall take himself to his house." This instinct is the same as the seventeenth-century East-Anglican witch floating. There are instances of the death penalty for witchcraft in nineteenth-dynasty Egypt, and in Assyria. There seems to have been no time when the practice of black arts could be carried out without fear.

As with today's mediums, some of the public could not really distinguish between good and bad, true and fraudulent, even though the rotten apples were few indeed in a barrel of clean fruit. Such is human nature that it frequently condemns the many who are innocent of wrongdoings because of the sins of a few. Of course, persecutions never stopped the practice of magic. The rituals became more and more complicated: "When the sun's disc is clear above the horizon, decapitate an immaculate, pure white cock, holding it in the crook of your left elbow, circumambulate the altar before sunrise. . . . Throw the head into the river, catch the blood in your right hand and drink it." Magic can be as good or as bad as the person performing it, but the aims are much the same as this: "Let her sleep with none other, let her have no pleasurable intercourse with any other man save me. Let her neither drink nor eat, nor love, nor be strong, nor well, let her have not sleep except with me."

According to most sources, magicians were treated at least with respect in the Babylonian and Greek world —and if they managed to be accurate in their predictions or performed rituals that had practical effects, they became rich and famous. But not so a little later in history. Checking the works by Theodore Mommsen and Harold Mattingly (*The Man in the Roman Street*), I discovered that the Roman State looked askance at the practice of the magical arts. Tolerance was not one of its virtues, for a monolithic establishment cannot afford to take risks, in the event that a magician gains power over the chosen leader of the state!

Magicians were punished in Rome with great severity. Tacitus mentions how Lucius Pituanius was hurled from the Tarpeian Rock and how Publius Marcius was stripped and lashed to death outside the Esquiline Gate.

15

Constantine the Great carried on a determined warfare against the black arts but exempted white witchcraft as a cure for diseases and the means of preventing hail and storms from destroying crops. Saxon law states: "If anyone be found that shall henceforth practice any heathenship or in any way love witchcraft let him pay ten half-marks; half to Christ, half to the King."

Magic does not depend on belief in it on the part of those on whom it is practiced, at least Western magic does not. Since magic is the setting in motion by the magician of certain processes, it is of no importance whether the person on whom the spell is made is aware of it—either the force exists and works, or it does not, for belief in it alone will not make it succeed. From observable results we know that people can be influenced by magic (whether we choose to call it telepathy, telekinesis, or whatever) and even our research scientists are more and more convinced that primitive man knew a lot of things about nature's herbs and plants that we are just beginning to rediscover—after trying to synthesize those same ingredients, instead of looking for them where they already exist!

In African magic, on the other hand—called *obeah*—the fear element is very important. In fact, the witch doctor will make sure that the intended victim is aware of the spell (or curse, as the case may be), and the knowledge of this heightens the victim's apprehension. However, the fear alone does not do the job, contrary to belief in some quarters. Just as with his Western colleague, the African magician relies on the powers of his mind and his knowledge of nature to do his bidding.

2

What is Witchcraft?

At a cocktail party recently I decided to test some of my friends to see how they felt about witchcraft.

"Do you believe in witchcraft?" I asked a prominent director who had done a number of science fiction movies.

"Believe?" he shot back. "Of course not. But I am interested in it."

A few seasons back, television talk shows all over the country were host to a rather substantial-looking lady from England by the name of Sybil Leek.

"I'm a witch," Miss Leek declared calmly, as if centuries of witch burnings had never occurred. Miss Leek, an author of books on the occult, is a practicing witch who once lived in the fabled New Forest of southern England, traditional haunt of witches. Miss Leek did not perform any feats of magic on the air, she did not turn anyone into a frog (although in some cases her patience was being tried severely), and she came across as an altogether engaging personality with great knowledge of the occult, herbology, and, of course, magical practices.

Witches walk the streets of Los Angeles, New York, London. Like ordinary people, which they are. Today they can do so with immunity, for at least legally witchcraft is free to be practiced. It is not yet fully socially acceptable, and even witchcraft cannot change that overnight. But I wondered: where did it all begin? Where *did* witches originate?

I studied the works of Margaret Murray, British anthropologist, and of Doreen Valiente, herself a prominent witch, and Raymond Buckland, an English witch now living in New Hampshire. Thus I learned how ancient it really is.

17

Apparently, the prehistoric people of France and Spain used various caves for certain rituals. Half a mile or more from the entrances, archaeologists have found campfire sites that had been circled by stones. There were pictures of animals painted on flat stones carefully placed face downward inside them. Perhaps magical rites were performed inside the circles to affect the animals depicted upon the stones, which had been placed face-downward possibly to prevent the power raised from being dissipated! In other places, clay figures of animals were found which had been pierced with spears. Archaeologists were puzzled as to their meaning, but the local people said, "It's just hunting magic. We do that every year when we want to kill wolves. They're clever; you must gain power over them, or they will get away." The researchers of Abbé Bruile and others show that some of these old cave paintings were used for magic, and it is safe to assume that the painting was done especially for that purpose. Undoubtedly, the beginnings of Witchcraft go back to very early times: if not the dawn of civilisation itself. Caves such as these prove that it was flourishing when Europe was still in the throes of the Stone Age.

We know that at the very dawn of civilization, society was set up along matriarchal lines. The dominant figure was the woman because she gave birth and took care of the necessities of life, the home, and the sick, and mainly because her skills were more varied and sophisticated than those of the male, whose main purpose was to provide food and shelter and defend the community against attack from the outside. The "finer things of life," then as now, were the domain of the woman. The matriarch developed into the priestess. The "old religion" of western and northern Europe was a nature religion. Unexplained forces around man were considered part of divine power. In this respect, early religion was pantheistic in that all nature was considered an expression of the deity.

But a priestess needed a more concrete focal point for the people she led. The image of the Mother Goddess was given a companion, the Horned God, who represented the male principle. After the advent of Christianity it became officially known as "the Old Religion." This was to emphasize the contrast. Even today, a person who is a witch does not refer to his or her faith as witchcraft, but prefers the term "Old Religion" or simply "the Craft." Originally, the Craft, or the Old Religion, was nothing more sinister than a form of medicine based on an intimate knowledge of herbs, drugs, the workings of nature, ESP, and simple psychology through the clever magic of poetry and the use of words to bring about certain reactions in people. These "earth people" seemed more interested in doing things for their community than in doing things in the service of any gods as such. Of course, one always must keep on good terms with the forces of energy they are working with, but the way in which these divine obligations were fulfilled merely suggests a rather down-to-earth attitude toward the religious element in their faith. The most important and practical principles were passed on by word of mouth from generation to generation. What deities did the Old Religion worship? No, not the devil. The devil had not been "born." Remember, the Horned God was not the devil; he was merely a male counterpart to the image of the Mother Goddess.

The Mother Goddess of prehistoric times has many names, but in antiquity she was usually identified with Diana, Dione, Arriarod, or Carridwen, even with the mystical Kybele of Asia Minor. In essence she was the "female principle," both the mother and the temptress, both young and old, but always feminine and always desirable—be it through physical charms, wisdom, or magical powers. Underneath, of course, was the dominating factor of fertility—physical fertility, but also creative fertility in the wider sense.

Even as with priests of other religions, the priestesses of the Old Religion often identified with their goddess, in the sense that the goddess would "descend" into them, inspiring them to act, and thus become temporarily incarnate within them.

But women lived among men, and gradually the man-priest came into the picture. He had a costume with a headpiece made from the horns of a bull or antlers of a stag. There was a Stone Age tradition that by identifying with and disguising yourself as a strong animal you would acquire the properties and virtues of that animal.

So now we have the man in a rugged, subordinate role to the priestess. The man took care of the group during the winter cold, and the woman was in charge for the summer.

Man's symbol of his rugged role—his horns—was later used as proof that the Old Religion worshiped the devil. I've never seen the devil and I don't know whether he has horns or not. I'm sure he doesn't need them. But I have seen some disciples of evil and they make it a point to be much like you and me. But the Old Religion had no use for the devil. It was and is one of the main tenets of the Old Religion that man is born innocent and whatever sin or guilt a person acquires by the end of his life is really his own fault and nobody else's.

This came as a complete surprise to me. I had always associated witches with the devil, believed, as I am sure millions still do, that witchcraft practices included the worship of Satan. But as I delved into authentic accounts of modern witchcraft practices, I began to realize that I had followed a "line" strung by the medieval, Church-inspired tradition that lumped all pagans into one lot—namely, that of evil antagonists of Christianity. In another book, *Witches, U.S.A.,* I learned how many covens or communities are flourishing all over the country, and not one of them worships anything remotely resembling Old Nick.

The more I looked into the existing material on witchcraft, the more I realized that Satanism is not only not part of witchcraft but its very opposite—and when I got to talking to some followers of "white" (i.e., benign) witchcraft around Los Angeles, I realized that they disliked no group more than the Satanic ones. To witches, Satanists represent an embarrassment, apparently, and to Satanists, I was told, witches are simply people who don't have the guts to do things "right"—use magic for selfish purposes without regard for others.

Through another source, I learned that reincarnation forms an important cornerstone of witchcraft, without which the cult would not have had its inner strength through the centuries of persecution. The Old Religion of witchcraft accepted what we today call karma, however, as reincarnation beliefs were among the early tenets of this faith. To be born at the same time and in the same place as a loved one was most desirable. The use and understanding of magic—as defined before—also was always a cornerstone of the Old Religion. Not just the priests could perform it; every initiate could and should, for witchcraft is a democratic cult whose leaders are by no means superior to their flock.

There were many gods and goddesses in the Greek religion, and Pan, the goatfooted shepherd's god, and Dionysus, the god of wine, related most closely to the Western European ideas of the Old Religion.

In the Roman State religion, the first attempt of a political church, there were still many gods and goddesses. Whenever the Romans conquered another country, that nation's deities were simply added to the Roman pantheon. But once Christianity became the official religion of Rome, tolerance was at an end. The ancient gods and goddesses were reduced to "devils," and the worship of other gods but the God of Christianity was forbidden. This despite the fact that Jesus had taken many customers from the pagans and incorporated them into his teachings.

Obviously, the hot, moist atmosphere of Africa will produce other elements of worship than those inspired in the dark skies of Ireland. Religion is not a "thing" that happened, but a human development of recognizing elemental emotional needs as well as each person's position in nature. Because countries like Britain and Denmark were remote from each other and from Central Europe, the spread of a Greco-Roman or Christian state religion was slowed down. The beliefs sheltered by the hills were able to survive better than those of the open plains.

The nature of the Old Religion was benevolent. They sometimes took from other religions elements that they incorporated into their own rituals. This is why Stone Age and Druidic rites existed side by side; the Old Religion was adaptable. Stonehenge was built and used by practitioners of the Old Religion and was already ancient when the Druids moved in and used the structure without alteration. Imagine my surprise when I learned about this fact through works dealing with the amazing English witchcraft high priest Alexander Sanders, King of the Witches. Until then I, along with most everybody else, had considered Stonehenge a Druid sanctuary. Now I had to look at the ancient stones with different eyes: after all, the ancient witches were there first, long before the Druids in their white tunics arrived by ship from ancient Greece. No human sacrifice ever took place there until the Druids brought this nefarious practice with them—dim reminders of their original homeland, the coast of Phoenicia.

Today's Druids are of course another matter: although they claim descent from the ancients, they are in fact a modern lodge structured more along humanitarian lines than an ancient and secret cult requiring human sacrifice. The only sacrifice today's Druids require may be standing in the rain during spring ritual on London's Primrose Hill, if the weather turns out that way.

The Old Religion was a cult "of the wise"; the Celtic language calls it "Wicca" and the word *witch* is derived from this. A witch is a wise woman who has knowledge superior to that of the average person. The male counterpart was the "wizard," not "warlock." No male follower of Wicca would be correct in using the term warlock, I learned, to my surprise, when talking to male witches. A warlock is a magician, a sorcerer. Let me make a point from Eastern philosophy: yin and yang. Opposites exist in most things. This is how schisms come about, i.e., deep-seated opposite feelings. The schism between black magic and white magic is greater than the schism that once separated the Catholic and Reformed churches.

While on semantics, the priestess and priest of the Old Religion were referred to by just those names, and the members of the coven were simply called that. The term *coven* comes from the same root as "covenant" or "convention" and simply means brotherhood, community, congregation.

22

The Old Religion was later called witchcraft. There is no need to denounce any other faith when a group of people have something good and true to follow. This religion generates its own energy through total living, not through guilt and punishment.

The following is what I have learned about the main practices of the Old Religion. Four times a year, according to season, man celebrates his happiness. This means that a person has had the good fortune to keep his fences mended during his life and is thankful that his material world is in good shape.

It is as wise to say a prayer of gratitude when things go well as it is to communicate with the power of your deity when things are not going well. It's natural for man to want to give thanks for that which nature has given him, and to pray for more of the same in the period ahead. Every culture has celebrations such as harvest festivals or May Day. The Christian calendar combines the expression of joy that Christ has risen with the hailing of spring and the renewal of nature. How about country fairs celebrating the arrival of summer?

The practice of dancing around the maypole is derived from phallic worship. The country fair with its merry-making is just a toned-down version of the Greek Bacchanal. Even the Chinese New Year allows the release of pent-up energies, including sexual promiscuity. Many modern psychiatrists will tell you that the idea in all these cases is that men behave better and more morally throughout the year if they are given one day a year to be uncontrolled and let off steam.

I am not saying that the four main holidays of the Old Religion were given over primarily to carnal joys. First and foremost, they were solemn occasions of remembrance. The coven would rejoice with gratitude that their lives had been good or prosperous. This was the purpose of the celebration. Of course, there would be some socializing and dancing and some drinking of wine. Remember that promiscuity was judged differently two thousand years ago and was a quasi-solemn occasion. (To read Asiatic literature is to find sacred love making and see instances of carnal union not necessarily "sinful," but primitive forms of religious

23

expression. Could the enjoyment of the human body be violating a natural law?)

The Old Religion celebrates four main holidays, on April 30, July 31, October 31, and February 2. They are May Eve, which marks the coming of spring; Lamas, marking the incoming summer; Hallowe'en, or All Hallows' Eve, honoring the incoming autumn; and Candlemas or Brigid's Day, the winter festival. Hallowe'en is the harvest festival and perhaps the most important of the feasts. On that night, followers of the Old Religion look back on the past year and its accomplishments. With hope for the future, they celebrate a year of hard work. Incidentally, "fertility" signified the desire to produce more from the fields and farms, not erotic activities per se.

Practical tools of daily existence were used for ritual symbolism in the rites. The Old Religion has taken ordinary working tools of the household as symbols of domestic and general well-being. A common symbolic tool is the broom. The broom denotes domestic order and cleanliness. A straw broom was always in the corner of a clean house. It was useful to fix a short stick. You could shoo away spiders or chase roosters from the house. It could also be used to teach the menfolk a little respect for the lady of the house. What better tool to use as emblem of domestic virtue?

Even when society around them had long turned to male superiority in its affairs, the Old Religion still emphasized woman's preeminence in the cult. The women who had "something in common" stayed together. When people have something in common, the way to continue it is to have a "meeting"; and this is the term most commonly used for it even today, not Sabbath. Just as in a lodge meeting (even something so mundane as Ralph Cramden of *The Honeymooners* and his famous raccoon cap) the women were traditionally expected to carry a symbol of their position. They used the broom. But when people not involved in these meetings saw these women come from their various villages or farmhouses carrying brooms with them, they began to wonder. By the time they actually entered the "sacred precincts" of the circle itself and

24

got astride their brooms, they had a bad reputation. When I was a child I had a hobbyhorse as a toy. This idea seems to have derived directly from this ancient ceremony. To me, my hobbyhorse was more interesting, but an ordinary broomstick would have done.

In the harvest ceremony brooms were used also to show how high they would like the crops to grow, if it was all right with the deity. By the action of raising the broom, witches showed how high, and thus implored the deity to grant them good crops. There is no other reason for witches to use brooms: They did not fly around on broomsticks. Persecutors neither understood nor cared to understand. There is nothing magic about a broom. When you use a broom as a symbol you are only trying to communicate the fact that your subject in some way bears a resemblance to the characteristic movement of a broom in use.

Each new moon is the beginning of a time period, for the Old Religion recognizes the division of the month, in addition to the four main holidays. In the old days it was unthinkable to meet when it was not a full moon; today, some covens will meet when it's convenient for their members, even if it's not on a full moon, so long as it is near one. The Old Religion explores the "hidden powers" in man, hence the connection with the moon. There is also a link to Diana, the ancient moon goddess, in her manifestation as Tanith, mistress of psychic powers. People instinctively knew that their energy had increased, because they had watched the moon increase its energy. A full moon greatly increases man's extrasensory perception.

But witchcraft is more than a religion: it is a practical method of obtaining certain effects or benefits. Psychic ability is one way of accomplishing this and it is a desirable tool. Many witches are psychic, and many are not, but the members of the Old Religion welcome psychics.

Christianity chose to take the opposite view. To the established Church, a psychic, a medium, was a dangerous radical, and if not controlled, had to be destroyed. A medium can become entranced in the full circle of a Wicca meeting. Then the members will listen in awe and with curiosity. The entranced member predicts the future of the crop, the coven, etc.

Anthropologist Margaret Murray, an authority on witchcraft, feels that the earliest witchcraft was connected with Janus, the two-headed god of the crossroads. It is strange that this deity should preside over the fertility rites, which were, incidentally, celebrated at crossroads. It is also peculiar that the same deity, Carefour, appears in Haitian voodoo. But the climate of the Old Religion of the West was different from the tropical climate of voodoo.

Summer weather and a tropical climate year-round can produce extended rituals. For example, gifts to gods (or "sacrifices" as they are called) took different forms. In central, western, and northern Europe, ceremonial sacrifices of an animal were replaced by a symbol. In Asia Minor and Mexico, human sacrifices were common. The Old Religion is a European religion: no blood sacrifices were ever committed. The idea of killing was repulsive to the Wiccas.

Yet, when you ask the average person about witches, he will either deny that there ever were any, or, if so, that there are no longer any such people. But those who admit that witches existed will often readily assure you that they flew through the air on broomsticks, had black cats as "familiars" to do their bidding, and engaged in blood sacrifices, primarily of babies! It was the late Nazi propaganda minister Joseph Goebbels who said, "If the lie is big enough, people are bound to believe it!" And so they do indeed, at times.

In high school a particular fantasy sounded very true to me. One day someone told me the story of the Hook Man. This man was a stranger to the area, who was supposed to have been a crazy man with hooked hands. There were many vivid stories of what he did to people who were in some way stranded or innocently walking in the country after dark. As the stories grew, people stayed inside their houses. But in truth there was no man with hooks. The town, county, and state police had no reports—I checked. The four or five local newspapers had not a single lead. In fact, this whole story was a myth created by some high-school boys. But it ruined one whole summer for me, because I was afraid to be free in the beautiful evening hours after dusk.

According to a leading authority on ghosts, people have many times reported to him the appearance of a hitchhiking ghost, usually a pretty girl, who stops a car at night on the highway and gets a lift into town. When the driver delivers her home, he is alone. Ringing the doorbell, and reporting his experience, he then discovers that the girl died exactly a year before. This story, with variations, has come to him with the names of witnesses who could never be traced.

Even the Ten Commandments tried to protect fact from fiction: "Thou shalt not bear false witness against thy neighbor." Unfortunately, much of the current information I get about witchcraft is myth.

So why do witches continue to meet? Why does anyone go to church? To influence the deity favorably, and to be seen by one's peers as a helpful member of the community. Both Wicca and Christianity share praying and the desire to talk to their god in the most dignified way possible.

There are many kinds of witchcraft, but in our civilization we are dealing primarily with Wicca, as developed in Europe. Wicca satisfies the spiritual hunger in man just as much as any other form of religious expression does. It is a matter of choice, and to some, the ancient gods speak the loudest.

But as the Craft was forced to become more selective, other elements moved in. When agriculture was no longer the only way of making a living, the emphasis of the Craft was broadened to include a desire for general success in one's chosen pursuit. There evolved a coven of community thinking that combined the thought powers of the members into something called a "cone of power." By raising this cone of power, the members of the coven, under the direction of their leader, could use this power according to their best wisdom. Also, healing was always very important— that is, the healing of sick people through mass prayer or knowledge of nature's herbs and remedies. These things became part of the Craft's program. There's no real difference between this idea and the group prayers led by a priest, a minister, or any so-called spiritual leader. Of course, a tightly woven and knowledgeable group of people seemed to produce the best results. Because of pressures of public opinion, witches began to meet at one another's homes. The best room was one that was big enough to hold about thirteen people comfortably. Stories about the strange powers of the number thirteen are being told, and many people believe that it is unlucky, or, on the contrary, very lucky. However, thirteen seems to be the maximum number of individuals that can be held together without dogmatic discipline (Christ and his twelve apostles, for example). Thirteen represents twelve and one— that is, twelve witches and a leader, which are a parallel to the twelve hours in the day, months of the year, and signs of the Zodiac. Many covens have less than that number, however. Fewer than thirteen people can comfortably run a Wiccan community. Even the high priest and priestess together are enough to do rituals. In general, however, witchcraft covens had a maximum of thirteen. When there are more than thirteen members, the priest splits off a new coven which must continue on its own. Rituals with more than thirteen can take place, but the excess number of participants are novices in the process of being prepared for initiation, members of the so-called outer court, and only thirteen full-fledged witches take part in the ritual.

The desire to be among the elite of magic, the witches, runs deep in the seeker, or even the curious. "How do I get to meet a coven?" is sometimes asked of me by people who have heard of my interest in the occult.

A famous talkshow personality (female) asked expert Professor Holzer whether she might perhaps, without realizing it, actually be a witch. Holzer thought it over for a moment, then replied, "depends on how you spell it."

So dear reader, if you want to meet a witch, all I can do is tell you where they are—you've got to do the rest yourself.

3
Witchcraft and Christianity

For nine centuries Christianity existed peacefully side by side with the Old Religion. But when Christianity became a world power through the state, it insisted on being the only accepted religion. This position was taken against all other religions as well, even though some of them, such as Judaism, had moral codes just as valid as the Christian way.

The Old Religion felt it best to exist in many small groups and it was not looking for mass converts as the Church was. Because the poor and oppressed, who had originally embraced Christianity in the Roman days when it was the religion for them and championed their cause, were by the eleventh century disillusioned, they turned in increasing numbers to the Old Religion, which had survived from ancient times. Thus the poor, the "country bumpkins" (Latin, *pagani*), the pagans, became the main supporters of the Old Religion and continued to practice it in their homes, sometimes in the seclusion of the forests and mountains—always in fear that the Church would eventually turn against them.

I knew that the Church considered witches their worst enemies, and I thought witches felt the same way about priests. So I talked to some of my Hollywood friends who are "into" witchcraft as a way of life. I discovered that they could not care less about what priests thought of them, but had no animosity against the Church either. But what about earlier periods of history? It is easy to be liberal and open about one's faith when it is safe to practice it legally, but how did witches feel about the Church in times of persecution?

I consulted the works of witches Doreen Valiente and

29

Sybil Leek, both "traditionals" whose families have been members of the cult for centuries. One of Sybil Leek's ancestors was a famous witch during the sixteenth century. "Why should we worry about a religion that wasn't even in existence when ours was already ancient?" the witches reply, pointing out that witchcraft antedates Christianity by several thousand years. Only when Christianity became a world power (through its affiliation with temporal governments) did it turn against the pagan religions. The Christian Church *in medieval times* could be compared to Stalinist Russia and Communist philosophy. Where Jesus Christ, the founder of Christianity, preached love and humanity, the Church spread repression and cruelty.

It was only when I talked to experts on the subject that I learned of the real reasons why the Church persecuted witches: not for religious causes, but as a matter of doctrine. Even the word *devil,* it was explained to me, meant nothing more than "stranger" in the Romany language. There was nothing evil in the traditional Celtic Horned God of the Hunt (Cernaunos), but to the Church the horns of the stag became the insidious marks of Satan.

While the Church was fighting the Crusades in foreign lands, millions were being killed by disease at home. The ally of government, the Church, preferred to blame it all on God's anger at allowing heresy to exist. A king had more power, if he had a link to God, and so the Church, as direct successor to Christ through St. Peter, made herself responsible for anything she considered evil in the world. The symbol of the devil helps focus what we mean by evil influences within man. Since a good symbol is useful to a campaign, the Church looked for a particularly threatening-looking figure to further emphasize the danger of evil. By church standards, any god worshiped by non-Christians or heathens was evil. Beelzebub was a form of the Phoenician god Baal. Ancient statues picture this god as fierce and evil-looking but not yet in possession of tail, horns, warted skin, or cloven foot, nor was it evil-smelling. These were added gradually as the description widened. The devil image was then associated with

30

the horned god of the hunt of ancient witchcraft, and seemed to fit the general picture the Church wanted to draw of their devil symbol.

Theologians considered the devil (or anti-Christ) a negative principle personified. A daimon, in Greek mythology, is the spirit of an inanimate object, the personification of an idea or concept. Demons in Oriental religions are demigods that live in the regions between heaven and earth and can be sought out for various tasks either good or bad. The early Church distorted the Greek term to suit their own purpose. To the Christian Church, demons were devils who helped mortals disobey holy doctrine. Psychic experiences were demons whispering in people's ears.

The superstitions of the eleventh and twelfth centuries are still alive today. In some Roman Catholic areas, demonic theology is still taken seriously. The Church was determined and used fear to organize: the concept of the devil was used to destroy *any* enemy of the Church. The Communist state likewise protected itself. In other words, speak against your neighbor, and you destroy his life.

In 1364, Europe was torn by the Peasants' War. At that time the Roman Catholic Church agreed with the feudal lords that it was heresy to demand better working conditions. The Old Religion welcomed these peasants because in Wicca all people are equal.

In *The Philosophy of Witchcraft,* Ian Ferguson tells us that Joan of Arc was the symbol of rebellion against occupying England and against the collaborating Church of France. Joan was considered by some authorities a Roman Catholic saint *and* a priestess of the Old Religion.

The Church put witches and scientists into the same category. Anyone who doubted that the sun moved around the earth was imprisoned and perhaps executed. Here again, the Church was like Communism: no deviation was accepted.

To quote Ian Ferguson, "All life was now seething with sin. The perpetual wrath of an almighty God slowly created by centuries of theological conferences fascinated and occupied every man of intellect. . . .

31

Beyond the citadel of the church there was social and spiritual desolation."

Instead of helping people work to make life on earth better, the Church preached that if you wanted to change your fate, God must be pleased *first*. Not by changing the look of the countryside, the poverty of the people and their dim outlook, but by stamping out *evil*. When concerned people tried to help the sick through remedies, they were suspected of evil practices. The Church and state were one, and members of the Old Religion were considered traitors. The medieval Church linked the devil, now called Satan, with the witch. All who were outside the Church were of the devil, and all inside the Church were of God. Pope Innocent VIII published a bull in 1485, which started an indiscriminate persecution of anybody remotely resembling a witch. A long period of cruelty and perverted values followed. As soon as someone pointed the finger at a person and accused him of witchcraft, he was tortured, on the grounds that only under duress would a heretic give out personal information on his "sins." Under torture most of us would say anything except something we are prepared to die for. At first one is likely to tell the innocent truth. Then the torturer usually makes up what he wants to hear. Consequently, you have innocent people admitting in writing that they committed treason against the Church and state. For this, citizens were actually set on fire while tied to a stake, or hung, depending on local fanatics. Sprenger, a so-called Grand Inquisitor, wrote a book called *The Witch's Hammer*. In this he listed the "signs" of being a witch. This infamous book was considered the guiding principal for centuries, and its standards were applied to hundreds of thousands of innocent people. Accusation was tantamount to condemnation, and the only way to escape persecution was not to be accused at all. Many of those fingered as witches knew nothing about the Old Religion; but they had properties their persecutors wanted, and as the property of the condemned fell to the persecutors, the motive was clear.

The Church did not permit equality of the sexes,

32

sexual freedom, or free expression of loving nature. It was claimed that these ideas, all parts of the Old Religion, were against Church doctrine. The position of women was way below that of men and the only place women could elevate themselves was in poetry and song. Even then, to write a romantic poem and have it talked of by neighbors was to risk some consequences. At this point, the possible ESP of witches was not under attack. But as the Church developed the devil image more fully, it became convenient to attribute all unusual talents or powers to the devil.

Some laymen still think that the members the Old Religion were persecuted because they worshiped the devil or pagan gods, instead of the one Christian God, and Jesus. But ancient witchcraft had only one deity, the Mother Goddess. The Old Religion never saw its deity as human in form, but thought of it as a great *spiritual* force.

Christianity has God the Father, who is omnipotent, Jesus, God the Son, and Mary, the Mother of God. The Holy Trinity includes the Holy Ghost. Joseph is considered a special "protector"; then there are the apostles and the saints and martyrs. A Roman Catholic may pray to all of these "deities." Medieval Christianity certainly qualified for the term "pagan."

Whenever I mentioned my search for psychic and other "unorthodox" phenomena to devoutly religious people, they would shake their heads and mumble, "But it's against the Bible." I decided to find out for myself if there was anything specifically forbidding interest in or preoccupation with the occult, both in the Old and the New Testament. After all, weren't the prophets forerunners of our great mediums? What about Jacob's dream, and Joseph's vision of Egyptian troubles to come, which brought him fame and fortune with the Pharaoh? Surely the Bible could neither ignore nor wholly condemn psychic experiences, I thought.

But the Bible has been used as proof in condemning witchcraft, even though there are only passages in it that describe psychic phenomena. But to take anything out of context is to jeopardize its intended meaning.

33

Some translations of the Bible *seem* to condemn the occult arts; the Church used quotes to justify the persecution of the members of Old Religion.

Two passages especially were used over again to accuse witches. In Exodus 22:18 we read: "Thou shalt not suffer a witch to live." This refers to a situation that existed then in the Holy land. Two types of soothsayers practiced their craft: the official and easily controlled prophets, and the psychics who dealt with ordinary people and could not be counted on to support the policies of the state. Moses wanted to protect his people, and hence the passage means "unauthorized prophecy is forbidden under penalty of death." The Hebrews did consult psychic sources. Moses, a diplomat, knew that government control in this difficult political situation was necessary for survival amid hostile people. Adapting this situation to different circumstances makes it false. The second passage is Samuel 29:6. This refers to King Saul, who asked his servants to get a woman who had a "familiar spirit," so that he could see her about his future. "Familiar spirit" is a direct term that means what it says. "Familiar" is common to a family or household or to a universe perhaps. The spirit that Saul refers to is in today's parapsychology vocabulary called a control. Saul was merely seeking a sitting with a medium. The adaptation of the Scriptures preferred to use the term *witch* instead.

When witches were condemned at trials, a "compact" with Satan was mentioned. Some of these incredible forgeries still exist. I visited the witchcraft museum at Salem, Massachusetts, to marvel at some of the documents there that accuse totally innocent women of things they knew nothing about. At the trial of Loudon, an actual signature of the devil was produced by the court, and duly acknowledged by the accused, too wretched from torture to contest anything. Sixteenth-century books displayed at the British Museum, which I inspected with great interest, even show exact drawings of the devil and all his "lesser" helpers, presumably drawn from testimony of the accused (and condemned) witches.

No witch ever worshiped Satan. Witchcraft does not

34

have a belief in purgatory or hell or even limbo. The members have a healthy belief in a hereafter where people continue their spiritual growth until they are reincarnated on earth for the further development of their souls. Incidentally, witches seem to have arrived at their reincarnation belief without any contact with Eastern religions. Man acknowledges the life cycle of nature: die and be born again. We have the Egyptian Osiris-Horus legend, and the resurrection of Christ. And so the horned god of the hunt, or male figure of the ancient religion, would die *symbolically* at the end of his reign. This ultimate sacrifice was thought necessary to ensure a good life the next year. No priest was actually killed.

As the Old Religion became a secret, or underground, cult, its followers were careful not to be caught. The code of behavior became more secretive. Except for those born into witch families, others were admitted with much caution. I have not found any accounts of outside secret agents exposing a witch coven. We have many trial records of what witches confessed under duress, but these cannot be considered evidence of normal behavior.

People would gather at their meetings, called Sabbaths. This communal form of worship goes back to primitive man and was more like a folk-dance festival than a sinister ritual. During the Reformation, Calvin burned people for the "crime" of dancing or singing. These meetings were presided over by a priestess and priest, farm people usually known to everybody. They asked the Mother Goddess to bless their crops. The meetings were held at night, usually on witchcraft holidays or nights of the full moon. To feel freer in the open, the witches took off their clothes and danced in the nude. This custom particularly upset the Church, and later the Puritans, and even today it is a feature that makes it hard to explain the Craft to a lot of otherwise broad-minded people. But the Old Religion also had a practical reason for its nudity. Witches believed that a person's body contained energy that could be collected and directed and put to use by the community. Clothes hampered this "power field," and

35

therefore witches felt that they must work naked. Eroticism did not necessarily help with the cone of power, or business at hand, although spontaneous love-making was left to the conscience of the individual. So the witches danced naked until it was time to put their clothes on and go home, until the next festival came around to let off a little more steam. They felt one with nature and they harmed no one.

In 1951 England's Witchcraft Act was finally repealed, although it had not been enforced since the nineteenth century. The superstitious mind likes to blame natural crop failures or other catastrophes on people they call witches, but the Restoration Period in England favored the concept of religious freedom. The Puritans fled from this liberal concept to the New World, and this should be kept in mind when one tries to understand the Salem witch trials. Titibu, a West Indian servant in Salem, Massachusetts, told tales of intercourse with the devil. Whether the girl was actually mediumistic or merely frustrated and eager to get attention is difficult to say. But like a high-school boy's tall tale, she started a hysteria that spread like wildfire. Even learned men believed that witches could contact the devil. An interest in music and dancing combined with absence from church services, not to mention psychic ability, condemned people as witches. All human behavior that was not straightforward and conventional was ascribed to the devil: the New England Puritans even persecuted the Quakers! Because of conditions in the seventeenth and eighteenth centuries, the Old Religion closed its doors to new members. Witchcraft was passed down from generation to generation and great care was used to disguise the beliefs and rituals. Even when the persecutions of witches ceased, witches remained shy about sharing their faith with the world. A true revival of the Craft came only after World War II.

Wicca is divided into four groups: hereditary, traditional, Gardnerian, and Alexandrian. Hereditary witchcraft has kept the Craft alive by passing belief through the family tree. Traditionals wear robes for their rites. Gardnerians stem from Dr. Gerald B. Gardner, initiated by a hereditary witch in the New Forest, England. Dr. Gardner was a writer who founded a witchcraft museum on the Isle of Man. The Alexandrians are those whose initiation beliefs have in some way to do with Alexander and Maxine Sanders. Whether or not a coven should be public caused heated debate. The Alexandrian view was that the tip of the iceberg should be visible. The Bible says, "He that hath ears to listen, let him hear." There is so much for a witch to say, yet in telling *all,* he may reveal nothing. As in anything, to have a direct experience with a group, a person must be *initiated in some way.*

4
What Makes People Want to Be Witches?

People want to become witches because of what it might do for them *personally*. Eloise L. is a physical-education teacher who was always called an atheist because her belief in Christianity was not strong. She found her comfort in nature. She wanted to find inner peace, to grow in spirit. Julia B. has tried many religions, Western and Eastern, but has yet to find one like the Old Religion, mainly because it fits in with her belief in reincarnation and that God is good and kind by nature. Marion S. of Nevada had a Catholic family who discouraged her belief in the unseen. Mrs. S. is the happy mother of two children, and frustration did not cause her to seek out another religion. Ted A. of Pennsylvania wants to become a solitary witch. His wife does not approve of his religion, and his night job keeps him from attending meetings. Anna and her brother Charles are high-school students trying to read all of today's literature to prepare themselves for the day of their formal initiation. Some people practice common witchcraft habits without being initiated. Mary was born and raised in the Catholic Church and school system. She feels that nothing that comes easily is worth doing; working hard to become a member of a religion such as Wicca might be a more rewarding experience than being one of the flock in Catholicism. J.T.R. is an English major at an Eastern university. He is trying to find the reason why he feels apathy toward the Church. He has a strong desire to live in accordance with nature's laws and not the laws of man. Peter D. has been trying to get into a coven by writing to authors of witchcraft books. Mary Jane W. is a hotel sales manager in Maryland and says she hasn't found religious satisfaction in the Protestant or Catholic Church. Sidney and his wife are students at a California university. They use campus bulletin boards to tell others of their interest in Wicca. Tracy L. of New York has studied the other major religions and decided that none of them met her emotional needs; five years ago she turned to Wicca as an outlet for spiritual development.

I discovered that young people particularly are drawn to the Old Religion, and not necessarily out of a sense of rebellion. They are interested in the personal and mystical involvement with the deity that the Old Religion offers. Sara M. of South Carolina is a young woman who feels that witchcraft is the only philosophy which is pro-life, not anti-life. It is as joyful and hopeful as she believes her life should be. Her reason for contacting a coven was to find a teacher to help her toward a new way of life. During grade school, the Church disillusioned her, she says; when she was very young, a teacher asked her if God would punish a non-Christian, even if that person was good. Her innocent answer was no, and she was informed that she was wrong. Later, in the confessional, a priest forbade her to have sex again without being married, because sex was evil. When Sara H. grew older, she was attracted to the "unknown" side of life, as expressed in psychic phenomena. She loved her Catholicism because of its magical qualities, but the dogma she had to study suffocated her. She found "her" God to be hateful, prejudiced, punitive, and anti-life, so she became an agnostic. Now she needs someone to show her the way of the Craft.

Albert is a social-welfare and psychology student in Pennsylvania. He is forty-three years old, and the father and spouse of a happy family unit. He would like to become a witch to further explore his bountiful life. Emma A. of Montana, fifty, feels a peace in the company of her pets. She wants a religion to practice at home. Her parents were Methodists but she always felt like an outsider. Mrs. M. H. had some ESP experiences but still needed meaning and purpose to her life; her husband fortunately gives her his blessings in finding her way to witchcraft. "How can I correspond with a coven and learn the details of their activities?" asked Emily P. of Louisiana. Joe R. lives in Connecticut, and, as he puts it, "twenty-five years with my wife have, if anything, improved my love for the Great Mother." Oddly enough, when he announced this to his wife, she thought it was a strange idea, but in the true spirit of marital love she has since accepted her husband's potential growth ideas. Mr. S., a thirty-year-old attorney in New York City, is a first-degree initiated witch, thanks to an encounter with a friend who was able to introduce him to the Craft. His wife has ESP, but she is not interested in the Old Religion. Mr. S.'s involvement with witchcraft makes him want to help his fellow believers through his profession.

Generally, individuals come forward rather than couples. A couple, however, might find it easier to be accepted if the quality of the bond of their relationship is evident. After proper training, these two can start a coven of their own, if they wish to. Susan B. and Terry S. agree that Wicca will free them from hindrances in seeking "themselves." Constance L., a nurse in downtown Chicago, feels that the pagan religion has helped her feel at peace with her own nature. She enjoys tuning in on people and can tell how they are really feeling. Since she's become a witch, her abilities have broadened, including her medical aptitude. Dr. S. is a thirty-eight-year-old former Roman Catholic priest. He is quite religious in the formal sense. He practiced communing with nature in his native country when he was young, and the desire for personal power led him to the priesthood.

The reasons why people become witches, or seek to join a coven, are many, but in essence they are: Dissatisfaction with other faiths (and a need to have some sort of religious expression), and the desire to become part of a nature-oriented form of worship, with all the "unconventional" trappings this implies, such as practice of magic, the occult, and psychic phenomena, and perhaps even erotic liberation.

Neither covens nor individual practicing witches ever did, or do now, solicit converts the way nearly all other religions do. In fact they discourage them, but are bound by their own codes to consider in good faith those who come to them who have the proper qualifications. I asked one of the California witches I met, if I would make a good witch—in fact, if I could join a coven if I wanted to. Even though she knew I was a Hollywood producer and probably not the ideal person to keep to myself the things I experienced, she readily assured me that my quest for the unknown itself already qualified me to a certain degree: If I were to study *their* ways, in time I would indeed make a perfectly acceptable witch! When priests and laymen, perhaps even Hollywood producers, are fascinated by a secret religion, something more than thrill-seeking must be involved.

Mary is a direct descendant of a known Salem witch. At family gatherings, she celebrates her unusual ancestery with stories of background and the persecution her ancestor had to suffer. But this does not make Mary herself a witch. Although she has ESP and an interest in psychic research, she is not an initiate of witchcraft and therefore not automatically a "real" witch, despite her ancestry. Only when the Craft is handed down from generation to generation does the religion come with birth.

Arthur is an artist who lives in Texas. His interest in the occult does not go beyond the use of crystal balls and meditation. ESP runs in Arthur's family. He has the unusual ability to carry on conversations with deceased family members, though, and through these experiences he knows that his psychic talent has great possibilities. In an earlier age, his talent would have qualified him as a witch. Arthur's psychic talent made him popular in his dating years, especially at parties. He learned that by thinking of his latest "crush," he could shorten the time between dates through, say, a coincidental meeting on the street. This kind of telepathy is not wicked, and is merely a form of human-to-human communication.

And what about C. James? His first interest in the occult came at the age of *four*. Mr. James was raised as a Methodist and found it to be a passive religion. Witch-

41

craft involves the ability to say prayers and perform rites and have what is intended in those rites happen. He, as many, felt frustrated and helpless when saying prayers, and they never seemed to be answered, especially when the prayers were for someone else, as he rarely prayed for himself. He feels that there just isn't enough power generated in the Christian religions. People sit, stand, and kneel while someone else directs them. In the pagan religions, all participate equally and actively through singing and dancing. The will makes the power rise, he feels. This has to be directed toward a central purpose. With a focal point, energy can be produced and become apparent to the senses. Mr. James believes that the energy that makes things happen in the Old Religion is present in all of us, and in all things.

Harrietta N. felt a particular attraction to Egyptian and Greek history. She was raised a Catholic, but at age fourteen she wanted to leave the Church. She no longer believed in God as people accepted Him to be, but in a "force of nature." She was in her early twenties when she read the book *Witches, U.S.A.* The mention of a self-blessing ritual frightened her, and it wasn't until she read of a self-blessing in *The New Pagans* that she thought it was witchcraft she was looking for. She liked the fact that her profession—she was a pharmacist —could be enhanced through the Wicca practice of healing.

Ben V. S. is a jolly man from the Midwest. He found his way to a group with Satanic links, but it was not to his liking. He began to look for a "white coven," but was not successful. Finally, he ran an ad and one person replied. Together, these two practiced rituals copied from various sources.

Linda is a self-employed artist who also works at a clinic for the psychic sciences. During hypnosis experiments she discovered a past life. It seems that she was a witch in another country at another time. She saw a dozen people holding candles, walking around her clockwise. Beside her in the circle she felt that there was a man with a bare chest. Linda felt a rough robe on her body and noticed that the rest of the people wore gray robes tied with cords at the waist. She experienced the sensation of being outdoors at night; she felt high and noticed that she was standing on a rocky plateau. The air was filled with chanting. She put her hands on the man's shoulders and felt the power go to him and her spirit fade into her present life time. The word *Hecate* floated through her memory. What is interesting about this case is her knowledge of witchcraft rituals, in intimate detail, which she did not learn in her present life. All this happened without benefit of books, lectures, or involvement with present-day covens. There are a number of such cases on record, where people, often without the slightest interest in witchcraft, discover previous involvements with it through dreams or waking visions.

Some leading researchers in parapsychology have even taken individuals who have had this type of past experience back into the former lifetime, and "awakened" them under hypnosis to perform magic rituals that they learned a long time ago. When these same people were later confronted with the actions they performed and the words they spoke under hypnosis, they were of course amazed at the knowledge they did not consciously possess.

Sybil Leek told television audiences of having had deja vu memories of another lifetime as a witch in Britain, and being put to death because of her beliefs, four hundred years ago. Perhaps unfinished business as a witch (or untimely, tragic death) may somehow be compensated by another lifetime as a happy, respected practitioner of witchcraft—and Miss Leek certainly is all that. In reading her *Diary of a Witch* I discovered that her orientation, coupled with her natural psychic abilities, has given her a most unusual closeness with nature.

Why do youngsters not even sixteen years old want to become witches? There are some mature and some immature reasons. "I was born on May Eve." "I'm a witch." "I was born with a widow's peak."

A lot of people who possess clairvoyance think they are witches because the occult reveals itself to them. Naïvely, they think they *caused* something to happen, when in reality they were witnessing a natural phenomenon! I've heard of people who think they've made people die because they had a premonition of the event. This is the result of fear and superstition. No wonder some people actually believed the accusations of witchcraft when their only "crime" was their psychic talent!

Another young person soundly states that she believes in the powers of the mind and is interested in the ancient art. On the other hand, a young man I know is upset because his mother practices "black magic" on her family.

The avenue to finding a coven is as obscure as finding a life partner through computer dating. It's difficult to know where an established coven exists, unless you happen to run into someone who knows. Secrecy is a part of *true* witchcraft.

5
The Witchcraft Scene Today

Social pressures, not the old legal barriers, have kept witchcraft underground. A witch is a pagan, and both words are enough to bring about a negative note in any general conversation.

Many people are interested in witchcraft as a growing concept of today's life. But to connect with a group is difficult and presents an complicated project for the interested person. One must read and gather information, hoping to hear of others who are interested in this subject. It is only when the individual becomes initiated by an existing group that he or she is truly into Wicca; without initiation, he or she remains an outsider.

I discovered that a coven of Gardnerian witches practiced in Long Island. Ray Buckland, who headed this group originally, maintains a witchcraft museum based on the more famous one on the Isle of Man, originally created by the late anthropologist Dr. Gerald Gardner. Mr. Buckland was educated and initiated in England and follows in the footsteps of Gardner. His rituals are always performed in the nude, with Buckland as priest and his wife as high priestess. The Long Island coven is a tangible group, even though some members are quietly establishing their own groups by now. Publicity makes an idea palatable. Buckland has posed for photos in full regalia, which consists of not much more than a helmet with antlers and a G-string. Buckland had a regular job with an airline that kept him busy between witchcraft rituals and supervising his museum. The museum has now moved to Weirs Beach, New Hampshire. The museum welcomes all, but the coven remains sheltered. The priest and priestess of this group are very selective and turn away many who are not ready. Meanwhile, Buckland's successor, Phoenix, continues to expand the Long Island coven, while Buckland is on a tangent of his own, called Saxon Wicca.

Herman Slater runs an occult shop called The Warlock Shop on Nineteenth Street in Manhattan. That is his *business;* his religious pursuit is witchcraft in the Welsh tradition. Herman is not of Welsh background, and yet he feels its perfectly normal to practice in this tradition, and he even lectures on it publicly. In addition, Herman Slater publishes a spectacular journal called the *Earth Religion News,* in which other witches announce their doings, and when one follows the lively exchange of opinions in the letters-to-the-editor column, one gets the feeling that witches aren't much different from other religious people, after all—they have their petty differences just like everyone else.

I understand that the Gardnerian tradition differs from the Welsh tradition as practiced by the Brooklyn Welsh coven in that it has three degrees, while the Welsh has four degrees. The third degree is being an elder and the fourth is being a high priest or priestess.

Our high priestess wears a moon crown composed of a copper band surmounted by a silver crescent. When she trains a high priestess who splits off to form her own coven, she becomes a witch queen and wears an all-silver moon crown. Her high priest then becomes the king of the woods, which is the same as the Gardnerian Magus, and receives a copper or bronze crown surmounted by a gold sun disc. Upon initiation we take two names, a public name for outside the circle, and a name for within the circle which is held very secret. My own public name is Hermes. Our name as a high priest cannot be disclosed publicly. Our rituals are very beautiful and very simple. They are a celebration of life and contain no ceremonial magic. We are the children and the friends of the gods, and laugh and love with them. We are not solemn within the circle but freely laugh and enjoy ourselves. Unlike the Gardnerians and others, all of us have an active part in the rituals and the high priest is basically co-equal with the high priestess. At every Sabbath the high priestess draws down the horned god into the high

46

priest. We wear robes and do not use the scourge. The circle is normally cast with a rod. It is opened with appeals to earth, air, and water, and is closed with fire. We possess the original "Great Rite" ritual and when it is used it is used by husband and wife or lovers privately and in sacredness and respect. We do not discriminate against those who within their private lives have found love with those of their own sex. However, we work female to male within the circle. Such sexual discrimination has never been a part of paganism as we see it. There is an inner court coven for the more advanced witches, and an outer court coven for the first-degree witches.

In Philadelphia, I found that Dr. Edward Turner is the regional director for the International Druidic Society, a charitable religious group that uses witchcraft to help and heal fellow man. Dr. Turner is a "respected spiritual leader" of over sixty-seven thousand fellow Druids, according to an interview of Dr. Turner in the Philadelphia *Evening Bulletin,* June 11, 1971. There are 197 covens in the Philadelphia area, with thirteen people in each of them. They meet about once a month. The organization is international and numbers five million in all. There is a supreme council of thirteen members that directs them internationally. The movement is especially strong in Britain. Dr. Turner explained that a new applicant spends one year as a postulant and meets every few weeks with one or two Druids. After four years of sincere interest a person may become a trial member by taking vows. "The purpose of taking vows and doing rituals is to develop oneself so fully that one can give of oneself. We stress emotional control because you cannot be a total person without some control of your emotions."

The Pagan Way is still another group, at P.O. Box 7712, Philadelphia, Pennsylvania 19101. A magazine called *Underground Journal of the Occult* is published by Rod Frye, at P.O. Box 734, Hampton, Virginia 23366. It carries articles on witchcraft.

As Eudora Welty's Southern short-story character, Leota, says, "Lord, yes, she's from New Orleans. Ever'body in New Orleans believes ever'thing's spooky." New

Orleans is traditionally a seat of magic, the occult, and of course witchcraft. High priestess Mary Oneida Toups, of 521 St. Phillips Street, New Orleans, Louisiana, has been granted a charter from the state of Louisiana to conduct the religious order of witchcraft. She is a black woman of great powers who conducts a witchcraft shop where supplies, books, and information can be obtained. She explains:

> I operate this occult-and-voodoo-supply witchcraft shop so that anyone interested in witchcraft may acquire the proper equipment. I am not in business for the sole and selfish purpose of gaining financial benefits from the profits of my shop. Naturally, there results monetary compensation by the virtue of my commerce: but selling the merchandise is not the end result. I am titled as Oneida, the Queen Witch of New Orleans—this being in that I guide, advise, and admonish other priests and priestesses as witches what is the established order of our religion. I possess a charter issued by the secretary of state of Louisiana and my covens and other witches seek godliness through the refinement of our being so as to qualify for the admission into the kingdom of God. So mote it be.

Of course, there are other witches in New Orleans, but Oneida's shop is an interesting place to discuss the Old Religion.

I discovered a quarterly magazine called *The New Broom* which may be obtained from P.O. Box 116, Dallas, Texas 75221. This publication represents the work of Mark Roberts and Morgan McFarland—the two leaders of a group practicing Dianic witchcraft in the Celtic-Greek tradition. It is true that all covens stress the great Mother Goddess, but she is not necessarily identified as Diana. The Dallas group also puts people in touch with each other, although it does not hand out names of witches, and can be contacted through *The New Broom*. The articles in *The New Broom* are varied and highly instructive. This Dallas group considers itself monotheistic, as their goddess represents the essential and primary creative force.

48

They are pantheistic in the sense that they consider every creation in nature a child of the goddess. They separate those in tune with the nature of the universe from those who are not. One aspect of Dianic belief allows for virgin birth. This Dianic coven considers itself "her children who strive always to retain the qualities of love, learning, giving and receiving, and delighting."

The Witch's Broomstick is another informative journal and may be obtained from P.O. Box 364, Lawton, Oklahoma 73501, at a small subscription price. The articles are by such names in the pagan "movement" as Leo Martello, Bonnie Sherlock, Gavin Frost, and Francoise Strachan. Joe Ferrante's coven is patterned after Gardnerian concepts and is the only active coven I found in Oklahoma.

Llewellyn Publications of Minneapolis, is an active publishing house in the occult field, headed by Carl Weschke. In addition to the commercial magazine *Aquarius,* it publishes texts of semisecret rituals for those already "in the know." "Lady Sheba," who lives in Michigan, is the author of the "Book of Shadows." This text claims to be a nearly complete recount of rituals performed in witchcraft covens. This is of course contrary to tradition, since such a book cannot be published. Anyway, information can be obtained from P.O. Box 3383-LL1, St. Paul, Minnesota 55101.

I also heard of a Cincinnati coven whose ritual was a mixture of Celtic Wicca and Kabala. This produced a rich, colorful ceremony that apparently pleased the members for the Cincinnati coven existed for many years. Unfortunately, this coven ended with the untimely, accidental deaths of their two leaders. Individual witches practice in Cincinnati, but there are no centrally located covens to be contacted there at this time.

There is a flourishing school of Wicca in Salem, Missouri. Its founders and directors, Gavin and Yvonne Frost, have been in the occult news through their first book, *The Witch's Bible.* The Gavin School of Wicca is, of all things, a correspondence school. The couple also travels and lectures on their beliefs; the school is their practical means of livelihood. The correspondence

49

course takes about a year and a half to complete. They send their students to a dozen lectures and after filling out their assigned questionnaires, Mr. and Mrs. Frost evaluate the answers to see if the student is getting the meaning correctly.

Here are come recommended books: Louise Huebner's *Power Through Witchcraft* (considered far from authoritative by most traditional witches); standard information books such as Gerald Gardner's *Witchcraft Today* and Eliphas Levi's *Transcendental Magic;* Hans Holzer's *The New Pagans*.

According to Gavin Frost, Celtic Wicca believed in "an overseeing god who delegates authority throughout the universe. Good begets good and evil begets evil. The present system is degrading; we must help improve it. The god of Wicca loves you and wants you to be useful and develop." Critics of Frost, however, point out that the godhead of Celtic Wicca is unnamed, and also point out that Frost prefers a male deity. He has named and defined it and therefore limited it in this way.

The essence of Frost's teachings, however, is simple: self-discipline, study and perseverence, disappointment with success, success without lavish worldly living. Three days a month the Frosts fast and withdraw from the world to prepare for the full-moon worship. So far, a student of this correspondence course can be initiated to the first degree. (Parental consent is needed for those seekers who are under eighteen.)

The initiation takes place in Salem, Missouri. There are no surprises as each prospective initiate arrives as the house guest of the Frosts, because the initiate knows long in advance what is to happen. The lecture material studied by the student includes a full script of the initiation service. First there are three days of preparation by fasting—only bread, honey, and water can be taken. The reason for this is that the meat of animals about to be slaughtered is filled with harmful adrenalin. A vegetarian fasts as a gesture of sincerity.

The initiation ritual is performed in a circle with candles burning in the four corners. Only spirits of good will are welcomed, and alien spirits are drawn away. The initiate is asked questions about Wicca and what it means. The initiate's orifices are symbolically sealed with water and the sign of the Celtic cross to prevent alien spirits from entering the body. This is very necessary in case of astral projection, because the projecting spirit then leaves the body unguarded.

The next part of the ritual is a sexual interlude between sponsor and candidate. They do this for a religous purpose, not out of lust, but sponsor and candidate must be of opposite sex. They may be people who have known each other for a long time, or they may have only just met for the purpose of initiation.

Next comes the symbolic humiliation, which involves what is called the flail—the initiate is whipped lightly a certain number of strokes by the priest or priestess; the initiate in turn whips his initiator. The initiate kisses the foot of his sponsor and is welcomed into the Craft by each person present. This is followed by meditation. The group then adjourns to a full meal.

This group celebrates high holidays and Sabbaths by Celtic ritual. They believe that the cone of power is raised through the excitement of the dance and through its sexual feelings, not through orgasm.

St. Louis is the headquarters for the Church of All Worlds, publisher of the *Green Egg*, P.O. Box 2953, St. Louis, Missouri 63130. The *Green Egg* is a newsletter that contains information on its own activities as well as those of other groups. Nearly all pagan groups around the United States advertise in it.

Chicago is a hub of occult activities. There are established information centers, such as the Occult Book Store at 651 North State Street, and the Bell, Book and Candle at 4749 North Pulaski, and El Sabarum on North Halstead. El Sabarum is the home of Frederico de Arechaga, a young Spanish nobleman, a hereditary witch and spiritual head of a religious community called the Sabaeans.

One festival observed by this group is the Venus Festival, honoring that famous lady who portrays love. This is an ancient Babylonian-Sumerian festival, whose purpose was to create polarity between man and the universe. There are several parts to the rituals. First the convocation, or gathering together of people. Then comes the invocation, dancing and song in which the gods are invited. One incantation especially goes to Ishtar (Venus) and one is to Mana, the moon god.

What you put into a ritual determines the results. God is a disc with two sides, both good and evil, male and female. Interestingly, this is part of achieving perfection. Perhaps this is the reason for some bisexuality in all people. When you liberate your head from the limiting gender, you can achieve a greater universal goal. The incantations call up the old gods, and dancing between each step of the ritual is used to work up the power.

Another part of the ritual is the communion, in which the people feast in the presence of the gods, and here the spiritual essence of food is used. The last part, the evocation, closes the festival.

Just as a matter of interest, let me tell you that the Sabaeans also celebrate the White Goddess, the goddess of birth without delivery. Thus she is similar to the Virgin Mother. Her pregnant appearance is used as a symbolic gesture to remind us that she is the goddess of reincarnation or karma. In the Egyptian Book of the Dead she sits in judgment of the heart against the feather of truth. For it was said that if the person's heart was outweighed by the double truth of the gods, he was committed to reincarnate. In other words, if you fail the test of balance, you must be brought back to Earth through the great discomfort of birth! Frederico de Arechaga says: "A truly wise person does not have to convince or argue a truth, they just live it."

Another outstanding group is organized and maintained by Gael Steele in Watertown, New York. In 1970 she read Sybil Leek's marvelous book *Diary of a Witch* and by contacting the publisher was able to make a contact of her own in the field of occult science.

By 1973, Gael had found her religion and had become the high priestess of a thriving coven. Gael has a serious outlook toward education. She comes from a good family and works as a singer; she is married and has four children. Like all witches, Gael believes in reincarnation. She draws upon Atlantic traditions for her rituals. The size of Gael's coven varies. There are no hard and fast rules of dress but simple white robes are worn. For certain occasions a floor-length garment without sides is worn over the white robe. The color of this tabard signifies a specialty for each member, i.e. herbalists wear brown, and the color of the cords show the rank, i.e., the neophyte wears blue. Here is a song written by Gael in honor of Diana.

Through the branches green and lofty,
I hear Diana calling softly,
Calling all who are her children to come and meet her
    there,
Come and celebrate the festival, May night is upon us.
Come, sing her praises, Diana of the moon.

Diana, our lady Luna, Queen of night,
Bless thou, thy children,
Give us they light, Diana Astarte,
Bless us with summer
Come thou our goddess and give us your light.

Another group, originally part of Gael's group, is the American Society for the Astro-Psychal Research, called Amerisyche for short. It is described by its founder, Thomas Germain, as "an organization dedicated to the search for occult and spiritual truth." The newsletter, *Amerisyche,* can be obtained at 141 Arsenal Street, Watertown, New York. It contains featurelike comic strips with reverse philosophy, book reviews, reprints of interesting quotations from other magazines, and question-and-answer games in metaphysics and astrology.

"In Wicca, progress is necessarily slow since first each step is given to me by extrasensory means and then truth comes via the usual sensory procedures," states Lillian Blayda, a practicing witch of Sebring Inn, Newfield, New York. During the past few years she was involved in gaining full control over self as a prerequisite for what she called "full-fledged witchdom." She learned how to make things happen for her, not so much through spells and incantations but by sheer force of mental energy alone. Since she lives an essentially lonely life, practicing, as she does, as a solitary witch, she has used her innate psychic powers to enhance her witchcraft. People come to her for psychic readings and sometimes to be taught the ways of witchcraft.

Most people believe that California has the most fertile soil not only for all sorts of occult practices, but especially for witchcraft. Somehow, the warm climate and the extreme liberties of lifestyle for which the West is famous suggest that California abounds in unusual people . . . including witches.

Well, they're right.

Take the city of Pasadena, for instance. Deceptively demure, even dull in appearance, Pasadena nevertheless houses four major occult groups. There is for instance Fred McLaurin Adams, the great pagan leader, archaeologist, and poet (not to mention artist), whose Feraferia group practices a unique blend of Celtic and Minoan ritual. Fred himself has adapted the ancient Greek texts for modern use, has written about them profusely in various esoteric journals, but is generally not known to the outside world. "The calendar is the backbone of life," says Fred Adams, who also practices a special kind of esoteric astrology for those who seek his counsel. Trained not only as an artist and graphics illustrator but also as a cinematographer, Adams gets high praise from Robert S. Ellwood in the latter's "notes on neoPagan religions": "A visitor to Adams' home in Pasadena is made immediately aware that this is no ordinary suburban house. The front porch is full of signs and symbols from out of the misty paths—wreaths, crossed sticks, painted stones. In the back yard, trees have been planted and named and there is a henge, a circle of nine forked sticks oriented to the pole star and the rising sun, like Stonehenge."

The main deities of the Feraferia rites are Kore and her consort, Kouros, Greek equivalents of Mother Goddess and Horned God. The Mother Goddess is frequently referred to here as the Magic Maiden, and she is of course ageless.

In 1972 Fred Adams and his wife, Svetlana, went to Britain to study first-hand some of the henges and pagan relics. Those who are fascinated by an unusual and highly sophisticated approach to witchcraft (which this

54

is), and who would like to read Feraferia's newsletter, may order the latter (called *Korythalia*) from P.O. Box 691, Altadena, California 91001.

Also in Pasadena is O.T.A., which stands for Order Templi Astarte, which in turn means it is a so-called Hermit Lodge. Headed by an artist/writer by the name of Carroll Runyon, this group is a structured, intellectually oriented lodge following in the traditions of medieval alchemy, demonology, and the Kabala. Their teachings are based largely upon a medieval manuscript called the *Lemegaton,* by which one can summon the thousands of spirits inhabiting the universe and make them work for you. Their rituals are splendid exercises in symbolism and magic, and they work in black robes, although the Grand Master looks as splendid as an emperor of old, once he puts on his ceremonial outfit. They also publish a little magazine called *The Seventh Ray,* and can be contacted for information (or classes) at P.O. Box 3341, Pasadena, California 91103.

At one time, Pasadena was home also to Sara Cunningham, the famous herbalist and witchcraft teacher, now residing at 1606 Twenty-third Street, Boulder, Colorado. Sara issues a correspondence course in Wicca and is considered an expert in magic potions, scents, herbs, and incenses.

Harold Moss and his Egyptian temple, better known as the Church of the Eternal Source, have recently moved to Los Angeles proper, where they maintain a sanctuary practicing the ancient Egyptian Osiris cult precisely the way it existed in pre-Christian times. The priests even make their own ritual tools and the language of the service is partly Egyptian. Although the ancient Egyptian cult is not a witchcraft form per se, much of present-day witchcraft draws on Egyptian material and concepts.

In Los Angeles we also find Martha and Fred Adler, who used to conduct a coven from their home but are lately practicing quietly by themselves. Martha received her initiation from the Cincinnati coven and later studied in England, and is famous for her healing services, which may include such bizarre requirements as restoring an aging movie star's potency through magic!

The Adlers can be reached at their home at 4501 West 141 Street, Hawthorne, California.

Another personable lady, Cassandra Salem, taught witchcraft in the Anaheim area. Sometime back she gave newspaper interviews under her real name, Judy Malin, in which she stressed the constructive elements of her craft; a little later she entered politics and she is probably the first witch to attempt to reach public office.

In Bakersfield, a lively and active coven called Georgian Witchcraft flourishes under the leadership of George "Pat" Patterson. This is a group similar to some of the Gardnerian groups in the East and is not as secretive or closed to outsiders as are some others. They can be reached in Bakersfield, California, at 1908 Verde Street.

Many college campuses also spawn witchcraft groups, sometimes organized into actual covens. However, these groups often depend for their knowledge on the books they can get hold of, and rarely represent actual initiation into the deeper aspects of witchcraft. So-called black covens are rumored about from time to time, but the term is a misnomer. There is no room in witchcraft for anyone practicing "black" or destructive rituals. Such people belong among the Satanists, although even among the devil worshipers there are those who are perfectly harmless, and those who are not. The most important thing to remember, whether one looks to membership in a coven or solitary practice of "the art" once one has mastered it or been initiated somewhere, is that witchcraft does not give one supernatural powers by the process of initiation. It does, however, awaken within one certain dormant powers, and if one knows how to use them and enhance them, then witchcraft is indeed, as the ancients claim, "the way of the Wise."

6
Talismans, Amulets, and Fetishes

Thus far we have tried to shed a constructive light on early human development. We have routinely explored information on man's religious experiences. A definition of "religious experience" is the process of worshiping a power greater than oneself. The use of power leads us to the subject of magic. The use of power also led us to some reasons why today's people are searching for an inspiring earthly religion. Perhaps we can join the parts of our puzzle by looking at the objects and then at the words of religion.

Let's suppose that there's nothing inherently wrong or foolish about worshiping man-made objects as *symbols* of the deity. After all, it is in man's nature to admire, even worship, that which is outstanding or pleasurable. When an art collector swoons over some particularly fetching painting or a fine piece of sculpture, he is in fact worshiping the *expression* of artistic talent embodied in the work of art before him. He is not worshiping the artist as a deity, but pays indirect tribute to the artist as the creator. The artist creates the work of art, perhaps inspired by a higher power; the work of art finds its way into the hands of the collector, who admires it and thereby transfers his admiration to the one who created the work, thus closing the circle. Everyone concerned benefits: the artist has found a buyer for his output, and derives artistic satisfaction from being appreciated; the owner, because he has acquired something of meaning and value.

So it is with holy objects: man creates them, inspired by religious thought. This inspiration may be paired with worldly aims or at times may have some commercial considerations: in the Renaissance, religious sentiment was secondary to a religious painter's fame.

There is great similarity in the way holy objects are treated by all religions. Roughly, they fall into two major categories: natural and man-made. Natural holy objects include strange stones, meteorites, shells, and other formations seemingly out of the ordinary.

Walking down Hollywood Boulevard, I looked into jewelry shops and a couple of so-called occult supply houses—among the astrological jewelry there were all kinds of talismans, from witchcraft symbols such as five-pointed stars, stars and crescents, six-pointed seals, to far more obscure symbols, including even the representations of gnostic formulas to ward off evil spirits. Most shopkeepers had no idea what the talismans meant, except that they were supposed to help protect people from evil influences. There were even semiprecious stones, mounted as necklaces, with magic significance, though the details were presumably left to the owner's imagination or research. In my own research, I discovered that the people of the Congo, the Baluba people, believe that certain cruciform stones found in the forests have miraculous powers, and they worship them as such. The fact that these are natural crystallizations is not important to them. They feel that the unusual shape of the stones signifies the presence of the benevolent spirit and they want this spirit to serve them. In Ethiopia, some consider the teeth of wild animals fertility talismans and for that purpose carry them on their persons. The teeth of elks, hounds, wolves, and other wild animals are considered potent talismans in various other parts of the world. Certain shells are considered the abode of the gods in the South Seas. In India, very large or unusually colored pearls are considered sacred. The North American Indians believe that extremely large gold nuggets bring the finder particularly great power. Man-shaped roots or wood formations were held to be gnomes in disguise and worshiped as such in Europe; in particular, the man-shaped root called the alraun is part of witchcraft. The mandrake plant also is said to possess wondrous powers; it must be pulled from the soil at certain times and

58

even screams when it is. Animals, dead or alive, have been worshiped at various times as sacred objects. Some Egyptian gods had animal shapes or heads. Since the people of Egypt believed in transmigration of the soul, the animals were not worshiped as animals but rather as *animal-shaped deities*. A true case of animal worship is the sacred stag of St. Hubert. When this sacred white stag appears to a hunter, he must not kill any more that day.

When it comes to man-made objects, the ability to create the object exactly as required is important, if it is to become the vessel for a superior power. Man-made holy objects fall into two categories: those that were not originally created as such and became, due to circumstances, holy, and those that were deliberately created to become holy objects and that were then consecrated as such.

An example of an "accidental" holy object is perhaps an object associated with those considered holy or in some way extraordinary by their contemporaries. An ordinary knife, consecrated for religious purposes, such as the athame of witchcraft, is a ritual object presumed to have superior power. To pagans, this or a vessel used in ceremonies in honor of the deity is a holy object. To the Christian, nothing could be holier than a nail from the "true cross" of Christ, or perhaps the shroud into which his body was placed. As for the nails of the "true cross," if all the alleged nails from that cross were counted, one could crucify an entire army. Obviously, proof is very difficult to come by. The question of whether the shroud of Turin is actually the piece of cloth used to wrap Jesus' body has been surrounded by controversy. The New York *Daily News,* March 19, 1970, reports that the Vatican denied "a certain claim by the Geneva-based International Foundation for the Holy Shroud, that Christ was still alive when taken from the cross." Apparently, there were traces of blood on the cloth, and the foundation felt that dead bodies do not bleed. *Osservatore Della Domenica,* the Vatican newspaper, reported from a 1969 scientific study that the blood found on the shroud had been caused by coagulation of wounds, and this could be seen by their color and consistency. Reynolds Packard of the New York *Daily News* remarked, "A key dogma of Christianity is that Christ *died on the cross*." The shroud of Turin has been called a fourteenth-century forgery by some, but many knowledgeable archaeologists have supported its authenticity.

Man-made objects actually *intended* as talismans or amulets are meant to give the owner protection and power. A talisman is an object into which supernormal power has been conjured by the one making it. An amulet has similar use, but it is worn around the neck or wrist and is generally quite small. Both talismans and amulets serve their purpose best if the power of their manufacturer is great. Through further research I discovered that talismans and amulets are either made in the shape of a sacred person or object, or inscribed with a symbol representing them. Each object must be clearly designed as to purpose, but there are also "general purpose" talismans and amulets to ward off evil. The most efficient talisman or amulet seems to be one that is directed toward a specific purpose or a specific deity. The more the purpose of the amulet is channeled, the greater chance it has of hitting home. The fact that the owner believes in the efficiency of the talisman or amulet has much less to do with the results than generally believed.

With the Christian amulet, usually a religious medal, crucifix, pendant, or perhaps prayer beads, the appeal is made to God/Father, Jesus Christ, the Madonna, or one of the saints. In the case of gnostic amulets, objects thought to possess intellectual or spiritual knowledge, the proper demon is selected from the list of possible demons, and the appeal carefully inscribed. In this way, the individual connects with the superior power.

Do amulets and talismans really work? Are relics really miraculous? Theodore Wright mentions an odd force that sets aside natural objects or man-made ones that are likely to transmit the original energies to later owners. A talisman or amulet or relic is a sort of container into which the originator pours energies created by his thoughts.

The effectiveness of talismans is related to psychometry. (Psychometry deals with the transference of thought energies from one person or object to another.) In the sense that thought energies enter the unconscious mind, talismans can indeed influence people. There is also the belief that the object is powerful and will help, but the belief and the implied psychological lift *alone* can't do it. The owner sets into motion within himself certain processes that would not otherwise be activated, and the energies freed within the owner are added to those obtained by psychometry from the touch of the object. Together, they represent a powerful energy source and when directed by the conscious will of the owner, they will protect him. If all conditions are right, talismans can be effective. Of couse, we must remember that many objects offered as alleged talismans are in fact nothing of the sort: in order to work, they can be neither mass-produced nor created for strangers without specific contact between creator and prospective owner.

Thoughts are all-powerful, but they are also elusive, though enshrining specific thoughts in material objects is one way of preserving them and preventing them from dissipating. As man's spirit is incarnated in a material body, so the emotional and psychic thought form is embodied in a material talisman. Just as the spirit in man does the real work, so the thought form in the talisman makes it effective.

The Christian and Hebrew religions have denounced pagans for worshiping the golden calf, heathen gods, idols, and inanimate objects. But the same Hebrews who worshiped an unseen god also considered miraculous the mezuzah placed above the door to the home, and kissed the holy scrolls of the Torah during services. The representative of the deity, whether in human or animal form, is no less holy to the pagan than the Holy Scriptures are to Jews. The difference between a miniature enshrined above the doorstep and the symbol of a pagan deity is minor. In both cases, inanimate, *manmade* objects are considered imbued with the deity, and are worshiped as such. The Christian relic, ranging from alleged parts of the holy cross to representations of saints and martyrs, considered miraculous by many Christians, is even closer to the pagan ideal of worshiping a representation of the Supreme Being. In the case of Christianity, the multitude of saints being worshiped relates closely to the polytheistic concept of the Greeks and is in a way more pagan than pure paganism (such as expressed in Wicca, with its one and only Mother-Goddess and Supreme Being).

I discovered that talismans are found among all peoples in all periods of history; no occult formula is more universal. Whether Egypt, Chaldea, Persia, Greece, or Rome—when excavations are made, talismans are among the first objects to be found. Certain Egyptian papyruses give the details of ceremonies for preparing the "ring of Hermes" and scarabs. Ancient authors have preserved the descriptions of a considerable number of talismans, of which it is impossible to give even an abridged enumeration.

There were talismans of all kinds—rings, engraved and sculptured stones, jewels, inscribed pieces of parchment and paper, worn on the person or hung up in houses, to which magic properties were attributed. The talisman might sometimes even be a living animal— lizard, snake, chameleon, or cat—of which the greatest possible care was taken; black cats especially have always retained a talsimanic reputation for bringing good luck (or bad luck).

According to Emile Grillot de Givry, "Talismans may be summarily divided into maleficent and beneficent. Maleficent talismans are offensive and intended to produce harm. . . . Beneficial talismans are essentially defensive; their end is the protection of the individual against evil forces and the attraction of beneficent forces. The majority of talismans still employed belong to this latter category."

An example of natural talismans is the precious stone. By their hardness and density, precious stones show that they were formed by extremely powerful forces of affinity and cohesion. They represent matter in its highest state of coagulation and compression; consequently, the radioactive influences that they emit must be considerable. Great care was taken to assign a special curative virtue to every precious stone by such writers as Aristotle, Theophrastus, St. Isidore of Seville,

Bishop Marbode, St. Hildegard, Carlo Dolci, Camille Léonard, Pierre de Scudalupis, Boethius, and many more. The Christian accepted with enthusiasm every pagan tradition relating to their use, incited by the importance accorded them by the Bible in its description of the high priest's vestments.

I read in St. Hildegard's Physica ("De Lapidibus," XVII) that the diamond, held in the mouth by liars and men subject to anger, cures these faults and enables those who cannot endure abstinence to fast easily; the topaz neutralizes any liquid in which poison is present, and the pearl is a remedy for headaches. According to Camille Léonard, in his *Speculum Lapidum* (Paris, 1610), the emerald, worn on the person, drives away demoniacal illusions, controls lechery, inspires rhetoricians with convincing arguments, and strengthens the memory. Deep-red garnets and rubies maintain the body in good health, increase the gifts of fortune, preserve it from the plague and poison, and reconcile persons antagonized by lawsuits. Jerome Cardan, in his work *De Subtilitate Rerum* (Paris, 1550), claims that the sapphire encourages piety, amiability, and, above all, *peacefulness*.

The following is a table I've found of the affinities of the seven planets with the seven principal metals and precious stones, assembled by Pierre de Scudalupis, in his work *Sympathia septem metallorum* (Paris, 1610), and also mentioned in Tritheim, *Veterum Sophorum Sigilla* (1612):

PLANETS	METALS	PRECIOUS STONES
Moon	Silver	Crystal
Mercury	Mercury	Lodestone, alectoria
Venus	Copper	Amethyst, pearl, sapphire, carbuncle (deep-red garnet)
Sun	Gold	Sapphire, diamond, lodestone, jacinth (red-orange zircon)
Mars	Iron	Emerald, jasper
Jupiter	Tin	Cornelian, emerald
Saturn	Lead	Turquoise and all the black stones

Precious stones are still more active if they are employed according to their astrological affinities and combined with metals of the same nature.

I discovered that "Solomon's seal" is one of the most famous talismans. It is composed of two interlaced, equilateral triangles, one of which stands on its base and the other on its apex; six points are thus produced, which are set, hexagon-fashion, in a circle. *Tetragramaton*, the divine name in four letters, must be placed in the middle. The Jews have an additional talisman that is called the Shaddai; it is worn by all Jewish children during the ceremony known as Bar Mitzvah. The divine Hebrew name Shaddai is inscribed in a round metal badge, and its use is of immemorial tradition. Sorcerers and Kabalists never failed to obtain possession of it.

I found many fine examples of the Shaddai in the *Clavicule de Salomon*. Let me describe one of them: In a circle, the face of the Almighty is seen drawn in a primitive style that is nevertheless very impressive. Solomon's seal is at the top, and around the circumference runs the inscription *"Ecce faciem et figuram ejus per quem omnia facta sunt, et cui omnes obediunt creaturae"* (Behold the face and figure of Him by Whom all things were made and Whom all obey). To the left and right of the countenance are the divine names Al and Shaddai in cursive Hebrew. This talisman is put forward as being of universal efficacy, and is thus described in the manuscript: "The face of the Almighty Saday, the sight and appearance of which all creatures obey and the kneeling angelic spirits worship."

There is an amulet at the Würzberg Museum that is crudely drawn on parchment and shows relationship to talismans of Hebrew origin. It consists of a Solomon's seal unevenly drawn, accompanied by six characters, the meaning of which is difficult to make out. Going around the six-point star from top right we seem to have a 2, $, 2, 9, h or n, and S. At 7:30 A.M. on February 9, 1749, this amulet was taken from the body of Anselm, Bishop of Würzburg and Count of Ingelheim, an ardent adept in alchemy, who was found dead in his bed.

We must also include the objects called "sigillate earthernware" among talismans. These were used in medicine; I discovered a large collection of them in the Germanic museum in Nuremberg. These interesting little tablets were made of different earthenwares, and they were impressed with seals corresponding to their nature, and in certain illnesses were applied to the affected parts of the body for curing. Stones formed inside the bodies of certain animals were also put to use, such as the bezoar, which is found in the stomachs of Asiastic deer and goats. Boethius, in his *Parfait Joaillier* (Lyons, 1644), tells of the many marvels of this stone; it protected from all poisons, venoms, and pestilential airs. According to him, one such stone existed in a toad's head and was another sure talisman for attaining almost perfect earthly happiness. Johannes de Cuba, in his *Hortus Sanittis,* has described a practical but elegant method of extracting this stone.

I would like to mention also that mysterious plant called the mandrake. Our knowledge of it is still vague even though many strange stories have been told about it. Currently we apply the name to Atropa mandragora; this probably is not, I learned, the same as those plants called dodaim in the Bible, which Reuben brought to his mother, Leah, and which so strongly excited the envy of Rachel. Biblical commentators regard it as the supreme plant of Venus, which confers fruitfulness upon barren women. Attempts have been made to identify dodaim with the lily and with various plants called amomum, calathum, and helicabum. St. Hildegard in her work *Physica* (libre 1, "De Plantis") devotes much space to the mandrake. She says, "It is hot, something watery, and formed of the moistened earth wherewith Adam was created; hence is it that this herb, being made in man's likeness, ministers much more than other plants to the suggestion of the Devil; according to man's desire good or evil may be aroused at will, as was done aforetime with idols." This Mother Superior points out this plant's odd habit of dividing into two kinds— the female, made in the image of woman, "species feminae hujus herbae," and the male, made in the image of man, "species masculi hujus herbae." I found

65

an illustration in Cuba's work that shows a double figure of the plant strongly emphasizing its alleged resemblance to man and woman. In fact, all the writers of the Middle Ages who have spoken of the mandrake have drawn the same distinction.

The word mandrake (middle English "drake," "dragon") is applied to all very strong plant roots thought to resemble the human body. A kind of narcotic can be produced from the root, and it was believed that small, "familiar" demons took up their abode in these plants. Mandrakes revealed knowledge of the future by shaking their heads when questions were put to them. They were once widely distributed in Germany, and were even utilized in medicine.

7

Spells, Incantations, and Rituals

The belief that magic works miracles does not by itself create miracles. Like prayer, belief merely sets up energy patterns that the operator can mold into a definite shape or direction. Some observers of unusual feats think that belief in their probability makes it easier for people to experience such "miracles" and that much of it is hallucinatory, an illusion, in which a person thinks he experiences something but actually doesn't. Belief seems not so much a positive attitude toward a phenomenon as a reservoir of positive energy to draw upon. I can believe that prayer works because of the emotional pouring on of energies and not because of certain key words or phrases. The words have meaning to the worshiper and in that way make his prayer performance stronger, but to the object of his prayer, it is the intensity and form of the prayer, not so much the real content, that makes it a powerful and very real force in magic as well as in conventional religion.

Now we come to a much-quoted and often-maligned part of magic: destruction of the enemy. I don't think mere knowledge that a curse has been leveled against one or that a sorcerer is out to kill one in itself induces death. Fear of the possible event kills only those who have heart defects, and the magician is not so naïve as to rely on *that*. In fact, the record shows that many people have died as a result of direct intervention by a magician, without even realizing that this was taking place.

When this is done for evil or selfish reasons, we speak of black magic and justly condemn the practice. But when it is done for the protection of the tribe or country, the term used is white magic and the sorcerer becomes a savior. How does a magician kill another person long-distance?

First, there is the African voodoo doll, the effigy of the one who is about to die. Making an image of the victim is helpful to the deed only *because it helps the sorcerer* to have visual concentration. Depending upon his artistic skill, he will make the miniature figure of his victim look as much like the person as he is able to. Then he looks at the figure and recites his incantations. Gradually, he will merge the image of the doll with the mental image of the person, strengthening his *link* with the victim. If he can obtain some sample of the victim's hair or nails, this will help even more. The belief among primitive peoples that such samples from the body of the intended victim are powerful magic and make his destruction easier is not entirely based on fear and superstition. Hair and nails do carry the "psychometric image" of the owner, and allow the magician to "tune in" more easily to his victim's vibrations. Thus, they are additional links between the executioner and his victim.

It seems that in modern times a photograph will do the trick. Remarkably, there are still tribes among the desert people of the Arab countries and India who won't let you photograph them for that very reason: an image of a person is *part* of that person. Proof of this concept can be obtained under somewhat less adventurous conditions. For example, Professor Hans Holzer has frequently submitted photos of a person to psychometry mediums who have then come up with amazing details of that person's life, even with information concerning secondary personalities linked with the subject of the photograph. In one of his recent investigations in which he cooperated with the police, a potential murderer was pinpointed by the medium as a result of holding a photograph of the victim!

When the proper moment arrives for the sorcerer to make his kill, he gets himself into a state of frenzy by means of self-hypnosis or aromatics, and then formulates the death-dealing act in his mind, with the miniature in hand, and in front of his eyes. He then emits the thought form of the victim's death. Since he *knows* where the victim resides, the message hits home. The victim has nothing to do with it. He cannot very well escape what he does not know is on its way to him. Thus the energy concentration containing the death wish for him hits him and will hurt his auric field. Sometimes it takes a number of these mental assaults before the victim is dead, but it does work, they say, provided the operator knows his grim business.

There are other branches of magic involving intermediaries, such as talismans ranging from jewelry to bones, from animal teeth to locks of hair—in short, any sort of object that is convenient and small enough that it can be carried upon the person. Some talismans are metallic and some are actual metals, but any object can be made into a talisman by a magician. Then there is the evil eye. Remarkably, it is still prevalent today among backward people in rural Italy and southern Europe. The idea is that the human eye has occult powers that may cause evil to a person by the mere act of looking at that person. Much of medieval superstition was built around the evil eye, and the accusation of possessing it cropped up in many of the witchcraft trials during the worst persecutions. To those who believe in the evil eye, a mere glance from it is enough to cause a variety of calamities, ranging from sickness and poverty to death.

The evil eye is involuntary and unintentional. Even believers in the power of the evil eye tend to agree on that: if a certain person has a penetrating look that he cannot help, and if that person looks at you, you must turn and run immediately. But even kings and popes had such afflictions, and there was really nothing a person could do about it, short of tearing one's eyes out.

Particularly penetrating eyes are one of the criteria that constitute the evil eye. Actually, anyone whose looks caused one to feel squeamish might have been possessed of the evil eye. This belief was so strong that people could be denounced for casting spells if they merely *looked* at someone directly.

It is possible that an ignorant rural population might seize some unfortunate wretch and beat her to death for having "looked upon" a certain person. In fact, even today we hear of stories of such things happening in rural areas of Italy and Mexico.

All sorts of countermagic have been used to ward off the evil eye. Two interesting ones I've found were raising your hands with the fingers covering one another and putting the hands in front of your eyes, and the wearing of specific amulets. Also, the protective methods must be used *instantly* in order to work. According to my research, some amulets consist of a human hand, with an index finger or thumb sticking out, or a phallic symbol, since masculine sex "magic" is supposed to be a potent deterrent against the evil eye.

I doubt that the evil eye is something people cultivate at will. Some perfectly decent people had one—the king of Spain, the late Alphonso XIII, and even a renowned pope. When a person with the evil eye looks at you, something happens *inside*. This "something" may be nothing more than a strong and compelling interest in meeting the person with the fascinating eyes, or it may be something more sinister.

For example, here are two cases I've found: The time, late nineteenth century; the place, rural Italy. An otherwise ordinary farmer had the evil eye. He looked at a local beauty accidentally, but in the presence of her father. The girl acted strangely. She was not in love with the man, but she seemed sick from that moment on. She had a change of personality, from a healthy, average outdoor girl to a fearsome creature who shunned the day and stayed indoors all the time. Modern psychologists will argue that either a biochemical personality change was triggered by having this man look at her, or the girl was simply acting out her erotic frustrations. I'd say that excess energy, carrying the hidden message from the man's unconscious, had stirred up the girl's unconscious, planting seeds she was unable to allow to grow to fruition.

My second example occurred in India some forty years ago. A Hindu holy man looked with fierce eyes at a Moslem. Many Indians have dark, piercing eyes as part of their racial makeup. But this Moslem immediately fell ill, was unable to eat, and blamed it all on the evil eye. A minor religious war ensued and people got hurt and even killed. Is it all fantasy? Something did travel from eyeball to eyeball and somehow cause a reaction in the recipient, a reaction over which he had no control.

Can a person really cast spells by looking at another person? Not in the sense accepted by believers of the evil eye. But making a deep impression upon another human being, to be followed up by further contacts, is indeed possible through the eyes. Occasionally, a weak-willed individual may fall under the "spell" of hypnotic eyes or even be hypnotized in the full sense of the term. But again I suspect the presence of an unconscious need for such domination in that person.

If you stand next to a person who has a bad cold you may feel the germs coming to you, but it seems strange that you could become ill because you glanced at him from a distance for a moment. That sort of sickness is in the mind of the fearful beholder and must be counted as among those that are psychosomatically induced.

It seems incredible that crossing one's hands in front of one's eyes wards off the evil eye and that wearing charms against it will help. But if you are a believer in such things, the amulet then represents a *fetish,* a focal point of defense for you; if nothing else, it will strengthen your conviction that you *can* ward off the evil influences. What is happening, of course, is that you yourself do the warding off by firmly rejecting the evil influences, and the positive thoughts emanating from your mind will repel whatever destructive thoughts may be coming your way from the one trying to cast a "spell."

A spell is a verbalized thought meant for another person in the firm conviction that it will carry out the spell-caster's wishes. As far as I can determine, it is as important for the one who casts the spell to believe that it works as it is for the one who is the recipient to know that it has been cast. Now, if the fear of spells were all there was to it, spells wouldn't work unless the recipient was neurotically inclined and directly made it come true.

For example, if a doctor tells a patient that he has a bad heart and is likely to suffer a heart attack, the chances are that the patient will have one, for the simple reason that fear, expectancy of disaster, and doubts about his health are potential *causes* of such an attack. A truly wise doctor would never tell a patient such things, but many upright members of the American Medical Association feel that they should keep their patients informed and therefore they do tell.

But spells involve other elements as well. I have proposed that spells and curses would work even if the victim was *not* aware of them. In verbalizing a directive, an action-tinged thought or phrase, especially when it is done with emotional force, the spell-caster does send out a force that reaches his victim. In *huna,* the ancient Hawaiian form of magic, there is a whole set of rules on spell-casting, and also ways to break spells. In a series of books, especially *The Secret Science Behind the Miracles,* Dr. Max Freedom Long describes the practices, which still exist today. Hawaiian magic is essentially the same as its European counterparts, only the terms are different.

Getting into the proper frame of mind is of course important for the magician or sorcerer. Some spells are cast not as simple expressions but under circumstances suggesting a good "act." He can raise his "vibrations" or energy potential to fever pitch through the use of potent herbs, drugs, or liquids, and also through rhythmic music and dancing. The presence of witnesses at such rituals is not only necessary as a source of additional power from the body fields of the witnesses, but also to give the spell the widest possible currency *if* that is desired. This holds true when a spell is cast deliberately. But if it is a matter of "impulse spell-casting," a sudden outburst of anger, perhaps, no such preparations are possible. But at no time did the ancient sorcerers rely solely on the fear of the individual upon whom the spell had been cast. The *real* power was in the way the spell was enunciated.

To cast a spell, I read, one need not adhere to medieval gibberish and concoct awful-smelling drinks or burn incense or do strange things. That much is pure theatrical effect and works only to the extent that the onlooker needs it to work. But the mental discipline involved is very real indeed, and conforms rather closely to what we already know is possible within the existing framework of the effects of ESP.

According to Emile Grillot de Givry, "two kinds of spell must be distinguished—the harmful and the useful. The distinction enables us to get a clear idea of what may properly be called the 'double life' of the sorcerer; a personage all-powerful in the countryside, hated and feared in his one aspect on account of the misfortune he could bring upon a household or family, but resorted to in his other when it was a matter of avoiding misfortune or assuring success."

Certain spells were profitable only to sorcerers themselves, and gave them advantages much envied by the common run of mortals. Those who wished to make themselves invisible need only speak the following incantation, according to a manuscript entitled *The Secret of Secrets,* kept at the Bibliothèque de l'Arsenal, Paris.

O thou, Pontation! Master of invisibility, with thy masters [here follow the names of the masters], I conjure thee, Pontation, and these same masters of invisibility by Him Who makes the universe tremble, by Heaven and Earth, Cherubim and Seraphim, and by Him who made the Virgin conceive and Who is God and Man, that I may accomplish this experiment in perfectability, in such sort that at any hour I desire I may be invisible; again I conjure thee and thy ministers also, by Stabuches and Mechaerom, Esey, Enitgiga, Bellis, and Semonei, that thou come straightaway with thy said ministers and that thou perform this work as you all know how, and that this experiment may make me invisible, in such wise that no one may see me. Amen.

There are several instances of death spells mentioned. Here's one taken from a manuscript at the Bibliothèque Nationale. In the Collection Dupuy (vol. 590, p. 24), there are copies of two letters from Catherine de

Médicis to the Procureur Général of the Paris parliament. In the letters, the queen accuses Cosmo Ruggieri, a Florentine astrologer, of having made a waxen image with hostile intent against King Charles IX, in 1574. She wrote, "Monsieur le Procureur, yesterday evening someone told me on your behalf that Cosmo has made a wax figure and dealt it blows on the head, and that the intent of the said figure was against the King. Cosmo inquired whether the King was vomiting and whether he was yet bleeding and whether he had pains in his head." Two pages later in the same manuscript there is a report addressed to M. de la Guele, a royal counselor (dated April 26, 1574), which reads: "The King's Queen-Mother has bidden me write you that the necromancer little Cosmo, who is known to you, has been taken prisoner and put in ward with the Provost of the Palace." On May 31, 1574, Charles IX died. Since his death was caused by an attack of mysterious consumption, Martin del Rio, a near-contemporary author, alleged that he was fatally enchanted by Protestant sorcerers, who day by day melted waxen images representing him, and that the life of the king ebbed more and more every time this was done!

While at the library I also read that to break a spell one does not rely on mumbo-jumbo magic but on the same principles that made the spell effective in the first place—disciplined thought and the ability to verbalize properly and effectively!

I'd like to quote the Gardnerian witchcraft incantation used in the so-called caldron rite at mid-winter. It marks the winter solstice and is meant to coax the life-giving sun back from its distant position so that mankind may feel warm again. The priestess, assuming the position of a pentacle or five-pointed star, represents the moon standing on one side of the caldron filled with spirits (the ignitable kind), and opposite the priest, who starts the chant while the rest of the coven dance around the flaming caldron in clockwise direction. They implore the "Queen of the Moon," that is, the Mother Goddess of creation, to give them back the "child of promise," that is, the light-giving sun that goes farther away in the winter and returns in the spring.

It is the great mother who giveth birth to him,
It is the Lord of Life who is born again.
Darkness and tears are set aside,
When the sun shall come up early.

Couples join hands and together jump over the blazing caldron in the excitement of this rite.

In his book *The Human Dynamo,* Professor Hans Holzer says:

> To incant merely means to implore in a rhythmical, orderly pattern. The superficial difference between prayer and incantation is that prayer may be uttered in any fashion, rhythmical or disorganized, since the meaning of the words and presumably the feeling behind them is paramount. The incantation, on the other hand, requires a specific way of speaking the words. Incantations are the prayers of Pagans and magic. Always directed toward a superior power, they are requests for action on the part of the deity. They may or may not include "counter-offers" on the part of the supplicant, such as promises, or sacrifices of animals or grain, as with some primitive religions. They consist of frequent repetition of words in monotonous tones or in sharply accented rhythms, coupled with definite physical movements. Some incantations are set to music and are sung. A typical Wicca (or Witchcraft) incantation addresses itself to the mother goddess, or to Diana, describing her beauty and wisdom, and then asking her to help the supplicant in such-and-such a way.

On the other hand, it is possible to utter an incantation quietly in the privacy of one's room. Incantations are based on the underlying assumption that the deity understands the significance of the words used. Man trusts that there is an agreement already in existence between man and deity and that this particular formula will be acceptable to the deity in order to perform certain services for the supplicant. Of course, there is no ready guarantee. Man must take the word of his priest or of existing traditions or perhaps only of his own heart. But his firm belief that the invocation used is the right one is a major factor in making it work. In this way the supplicant has done something positive about the situation.

I was very interested and wanted to find out what exactly works in an incantation. I have personally witnessed incantations both by groups and by individuals, and, at the very least, a sense of elevation and purification of mind and body follows the ritual performance of the incantation. Negative thinking is replaced by confidence. Even more, though, partial or even total identification with the deity may occur. In such a state of near-ecstasy, the supplicant imagines himself possessed of divine powers and goes about solving his problems accordingly. How can we say with certainty that some divine element does not indeed enter the mind and body of the supplicant at that point? If we accept the philosophy that God is within us at all times, it may well be that incantations awaken such dormant sparks of divinity within and make them work for us, together with our own human impulses. Properly formulated incantations, voiced at the height of the emotional wave that accompanies rituals, have a degree of effectiveness.

Invocations and evocations are closely related to incantations. All three are directed toward a specific deity, or, with some pagan religions, "demon." An incantation is a simple prayer for help, but an invocation resembles an order more than a prayer. An invocation uses polite language, contains praise of the invoked power, and at the same time commands the invoked power to perform the requested service without fail. In Judaism and Christianity invocations serve primarily as instruments of revenge or punishment. The wrath of God or of one of the saints may be called down upon someone who has wronged the supplicant. Neither Hebrew nor Christian religion invokes the deity for positive purposes; they prefer to use prayer. This may be due to the Judao-Christian God being essentially a terrifying father figure with whom one does not toy. Invocations are used primarily in pagan religions and magic cults because the pagan gods are viewed as friends and familiars and can be *made* to serve, whether willing or not.

The term *invocation* means to call down upon one-self, to call in; *evocation* means to call out, to call from within to the outside, to bring forth.

Evocation is used in magical practices primarily to *bring out* from within the slumbering magical qualities of the *app*licant, who is now no longer a *supp*licant. The magician—not the stage magician, but the esoteric magician—is fully aware of his superior powers. When he evokes a deity or demon, he does so from a position of equality. He knows the magic formulas, he knows what must be done to make such and such a power obey the call. Magicians appeal to the spirits within everything, from inanimate objects to the stars, from humans to animals and plants, and to the deities and demons of the underworld. To the magician, there is no such thing as spiritless matter; everything existing has within its innermost core a spirit or demon guiding it. In magical evocation the forces within the magician as well as the forces drawn down from the universe combine to make the operation possible. The secret of magic is to find a way to evoke that spirit, and make it obedient to the magician.

The term *ritual* derives from the Latin word *ritus,* meaning the proper way, the *right* way. At all times in all cultures, great importance has been attached to the proper way of performing religious ceremonies. The origin of ritual lies deeply buried in man's past but relates to "sympathetic magic," the enactment of certain scenes to *induce* nature (or the deities) to make it reality. Sympathetic magic presents what man wants done in graphic, visual terms. For example, when the priest raises the host toward the altar, the act is clearly a means of showing the worshipers what it looks like and where it belongs in relation to the altar. But the esoteric meaning also conveys the thought that the priest puts the deity above his earthly self, and in elevating his hands along with the host he reaches out to the higher spheres.

There are ten elements in a ritual. If even one of these elements is not attended to, the ritual may fail. In the opinion of priests performing rituals, only the *entire* range of elements assures proper results.

Every religion uses the calendar theory that *time* is of the utmost importance. Christians insist on feast days, rather than feast hours or minutes. Pagan religions work only if they observe time to the nearest minute.

Place is second. With pagans, the outdoors or a pagan temple is preferred, although in modern times pagan rituals have been performed in living rooms as well as in the great outdoors. With Christians, Hebrews, Buddhists, and others, a church or temple is the preferred place of worship. A quiet, inspiring location is more likely to be used for a ritual because it supplies a proper mood and atmosphere. That is also why there is so much art in churches and temples.

Costume of the officiating priest or priestess is next. There are deep symbolic reasons behind every piece of clothing worn by a priest or priestess. In Christianity, the robe worn by priests is carefully prescribed by Church law. Depending upon the reasons for the ritual, simplicity or majesty is emphasized in the clothing. For specific reasons, monks wear rough clothing, and bishops ornate robes. Each expresses a different *aspect* of the religion. In the pagan religions, the priest's body adornment is dominated by symbolic representations of nature and of the deities expressing that oneness with nature. The colors of the robe are carefully chosen to coincide with the particular ritual and the time of the year in which it is performed.

Tools, or the instruments used in the performance of a ritual, come next. In the Hebrew faith, candles and leather strips wound around the wrists, known as phylacteries, are used by the Orthodox. In Christianity, the Bible, the crucifix, the chalice, the bell, the fisherman's ring, and the stole are the chief tools of the officiating priest. In pagan religions, various simple tools are used, such as the knife called *athame,* the whip, the wand and the sword, the chalice, and the cord or girdle. Eastern religions use sacred talismans, representations in metal, stone, or wood, of their deities as part of the ritual. In fact, any man-made object consecrated to a particular religious purpose may be considered a tool of ritual provided it is made for that purpose and used during the actual ceremony.

In Search of
Magic
and
Witchcraft

Modern
Witchcraft

The Old Religion was a cult of the wise.
The Celtic language called it Wicca.
This is a modern-day magic circle cast by
British Wicca High Priest Alex Sanders
which includes tarot as well as traditional
tools of witchcraft, such as a wand,
chalice and candle.

London High Priestess Maxine blessing
Alex Sanders and coven during a ceremony.

High Priest Alex Sanders at
Stonehenge on Hallowe'en
imploring the goddess for
hints of the year
ahead; while the coven does
a reel in the background.

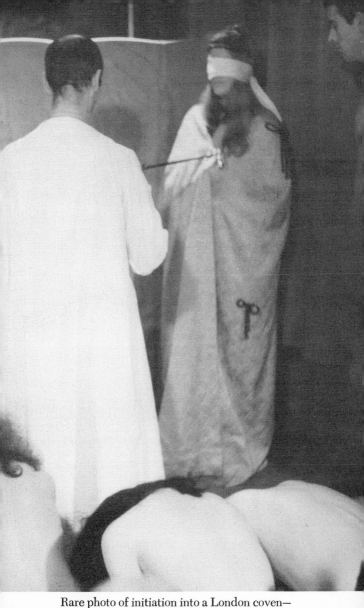

Rare photo of initiation into a London coven—
the novice is challenged by High Priest Sanders at the
"portals" of the circle.

Theurgic seal, or symbol, used in demonology
at a Cincinnati coven headquarters, no longer active.

Grandmaster of Ordo Templi Astart, a hermetic lodge
in Pasadena, Calif., opening a secret
rite ceremony. This lodge follows the traditions of
medieval alchemy, demonology, and the Kabala.

Voodoo

Papa Joi, one of the five most powerful
Hungans (Priests) in Haiti, stands over voodoo cross.
Note the jeweled straw hat in the background,
placed there for a favored spirit.

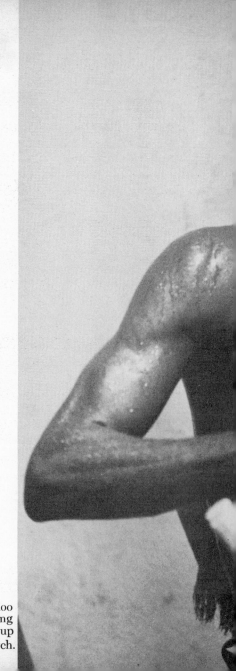

A voodoo
drummer working
the people up
to a feverish pitch.

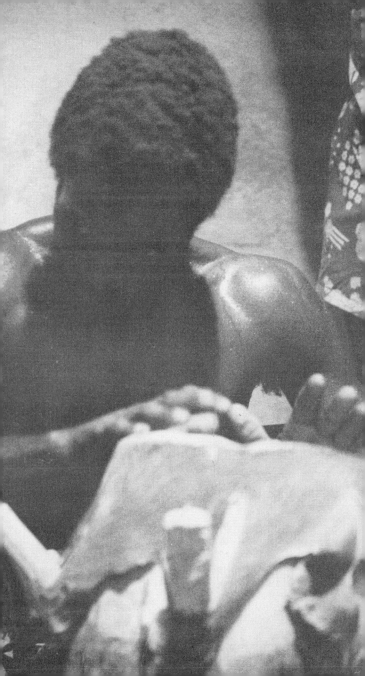

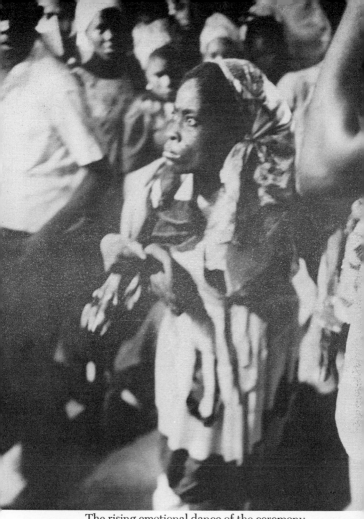
The rising emotional dance of the ceremony produces a state of possession in this woman. She becomes the tool of the spirit.

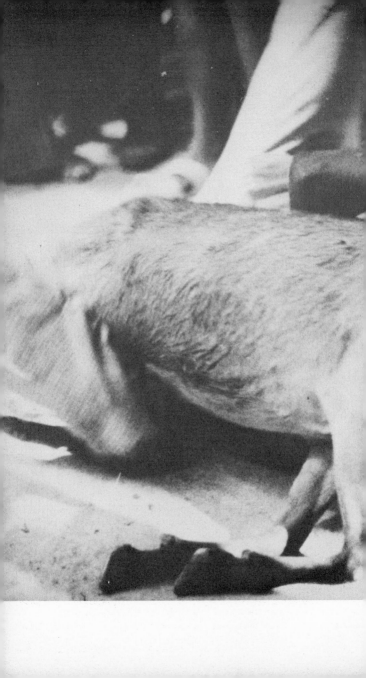

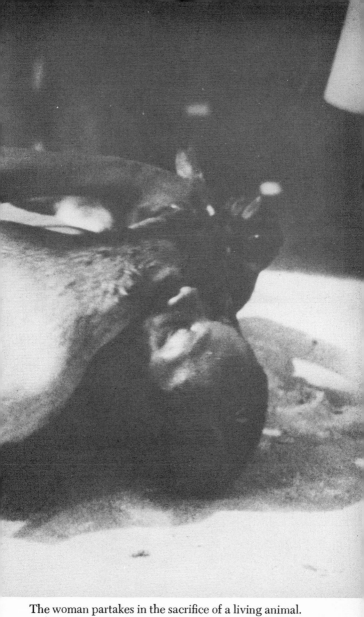

The woman partakes in the sacrifice of a living animal.

Exorcism

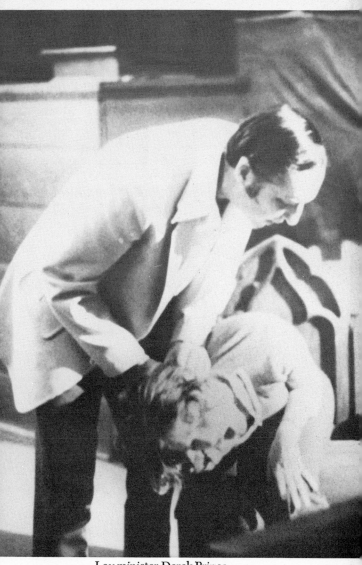
Lay minister Derek Prince
was called to a church in Eatonton, Ga., to
exorcise the demon in Rachel E. Johnson.

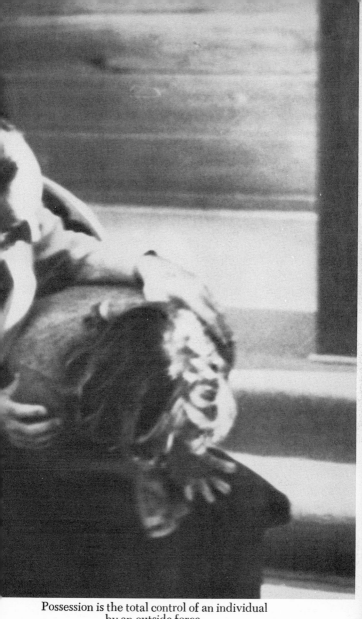

Possession is the total control of an individual
by an outside force.

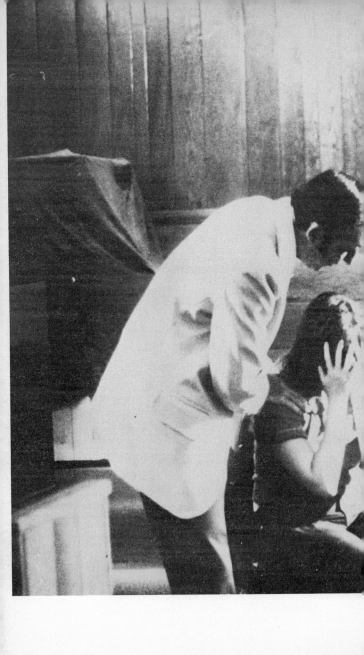

Reverend Prince's belief in his own success
paid off after 3½ hours.

Medicine
Men

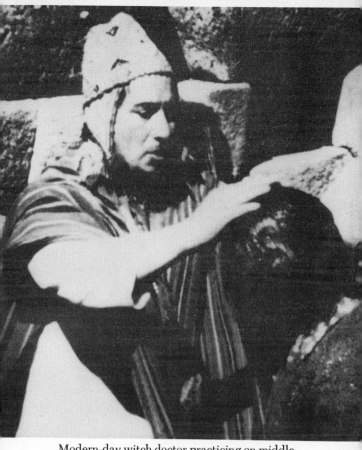

Modern-day witch doctor practicing on middle class patients in Cuzco, Peru. He uses incantation medicine and the healing waters from Incan wells.

Tapestry of an ancient
Peruvian medicine man.

The modern American
medicine man is
the primitive equivalent
of the doctor and the
psychiatrist. This medicine
man is digging up roots
for a ceremony to welcome
the birth of a newborn
baby—an Indian
baptism.

Magical
Energy

Through meditation, concentration, and levitation, these Indian fakirs lifted a 125-pound stone with one finger each.

The Sundance is another
purification ritual performed by the American
Rosebud Sioux. A leather strip is
tied through this man's skin and, in a high-pitched
frenzy, is ripped open.
Purification of the mind and body follows.

Next come *aromatics,* including incense. They set the emotional climate of the place of worship and influence the mood of the worshipers. Aromatics used in religious rituals are never strong enough to cause inebriation or other forms of altered consciousness, but they help relax the worshipers and create a receptive atmosphere. Among the best-known aromatics used are myrrh, frankincense, jasmine, and sandalwood.

Oils, symbolic of life eternal, are used by most religions both for burning in specially designed lamps and for anointing. The thought behind the use of oils for anointing seems to be that oil sticks to whatever one puts it upon. In addition, it was thought that the oil, pressed from plants and the life juice of those plants, would represent the life force in man and thus the act of anointing would become one of sanctifying or consecrating the recipient with part of a sacred life force.

The use of *foods,* such as wine and bread, is also common to most religions for communion. It is purely symbolic, as neither wine nor bread have any inherent magical qualities. However, in African voodoo, there are feasts in honor of the deity as part of the African religious ritual. Most of these African meals are heavily spiced and have mild psychedelic effects.

Sounds are also important to many rituals. Sacred music in church is one of the pillars of the ritual; it creates a mood of solemnity. Drums and guns are used in Eastern religions to start and end a ritual, and also to summon the deities. Haitian voodoo is unthinkable without continuous use of small drums, even during the ceremony itself and while the priest performs verbal magic. Only intellectually oriented Protestants do without the use of music in their rituals, except for fundamentalist offshoots.

Movements, including dance, are part of the rituals of many religions. In the Christian religion, the movement of the priest is carefully prescribed by the scriptures and by the interpretations of Christian doctrine. Only in very recent times have such elements as contemporary music and ritual dance been introduced into the service to win back some of the young people who have wandered away from the Church.

In some Hebraic sects, such as the Chassidic, joyous dancing is part of the ritual. In Hinduism, dance is so much an integral part of the ritual that temple dancers are trained in large schools adjacent to the temples themselves. The movement of the temple dancers is as carefully prescribed as all other parts of the ritual. Islam, considered the most intellectual of all religions, frowns upon joyous expression of human desires, but there are sects that practice ritual dancing, such as the Dervishes. In Wicca, ritual dancing is used as a means of increasing the outpour of psychic energies. In the Sabaean pagan religion, extended periods of fast dancing are also used. Dancing gives a feeling of abandonment and detachment necessary for the performance of the ritual, but it also creates energies that the officiating priest or priestess can use as a power reserve.

Last but not least, the *words* make the ritual work. They may be spoken or sung, but they are very carefully put together. Not only are the words chosen for specific effects, but the timing and placement of the words in relation to the other nine elements is very important.

8

Mediterranean Magic Cults in Modern America

My research has made me aware of a revival of paganism, though I found that the return to pagan ideals made small headway during the two world wars. Preoccupation with material welfare, industrial and scientific progress beyond hopes, and a general orientation toward more tangible goals kept large masses from delving into the advantages and delights of the pagan life. But the 1950s and 1960s brought disillusionment with the various forms of Establishment government, Establishment religion, even Establishment philosophy. The young especially looked toward other paths to find themselves in their relationship to the deity. Simultaneously with the rising interest in the occult, a new wave of seekers in the pagan way spread throughout the Western world. Not only a revival of an interest in witchcraft, or the Celtic form of the Old Religion, but other pagan cults of Mediterranean or Hebrew origin fascinate the young and those of nonconformist leanings among all age groups.

Some years ago I became familiar with a group called Feraferia, which I mentioned in Chapter 5. This group described itself as "a love culture for wilderness," and ecological concepts were at the core of its teachings long before ecology became a household term in America, long before an alarmed country finally became aware of the need to preserve what is left of our natural heritage. Its leader, Fred Adams, lives and breathes preservation, return to the natural state of living, the planting of new trees, the saving of city areas from destruction, the cleansing and purification of rural areas. These are as important to Fred and his group as are the more involved pagan rituals, worshiping the "magic maiden," the symbolic deity representing the female principle in nature, creation, the spark within.

Feraferia is far more than witchcraft and does not even use that term to describe itself. Where Wicca and male-oriented witchcraft groups worship in rites to express their desires symbolically and, through incantations, try to change things for themselves or for others, Feraferia goes beyond the ritual: it enacts what it stands for in actual nature. Weather permitting, there are side trips into the wilderness where the group communes with nature. There are attempts at restoring neglected areas to their natural appearance, and, as a consequence, even the ritual is far more realistic and vital than the rituals of many intellectually inclined pagan groups.

I was fascinated by Feraferia. I found it vibrant and love-oriented. Feraferia does not contain a single negative ritual. While there are some protective incantations and spells in Wicca to ward off enemies or evil human beings, Feraferia has none. This group believes that the positive force alone will protect them. All ritualistic activity in Feraferia revolves around the ancient Greek calendar, based upon thirteen months of twenty-eight days each. Every moment is carefully charted by Fred Adams in an elaborate and intricate calendar, which he himself constructed. The goal for the men and women in Feraferia is to be completely in tune with what goes on in nature. They carefully calculate the right moment for whatever they are undertaking. As a result, their lives become wholly attuned to natural living, bringing them, Feraferia believes, total immersion, total fulfillment, and a way of life different from the city-bred destructiveness and ill health to which Fred and his friends ascribe so many of today's ills.

The cults of Artemis, the Diana of the Celtic world, and of Dionysus involved ancient Greek witchcraft practices. Interestingly, their services were called mysteries—mysteries as in mysticism.

Some things are veiled and then disclosed to the initiate at the proper time. Others must remain hidden forever. Entering the mysteries is a gradual and emotional experience. In so closely knit a group as Feraferia, even the introductory step is not possible until the initiate has been properly prepared through studies and above all through the understanding of the ritual meaning inherent in Feraferia.

In 1967, Fred Adams stated in his writing on the principles of this group:

Wilderness is the elusive quick of all spontaneous delicately urging life. The only way to re-unite mankind is to re-unite mankind with nature. Man will become humane toward man only when he becomes humane toward all nature. The inner nature of man has been disastrously severed from the all-enveloping nature of wilderness. The vital link between visionary nature within and ecological nature without is poetry.

All pagan religions equate nature forces with various deities. In worshiping a seemingly independent deity existing somewhere outside oneself, one is in fact drawing upon one's inner forces, and, in doing so, sparkplugs those forces into performing for oneself. Since the ancient gods are merely various aspects of nature, and since within us we have aspects of these gods, there may be many names by which one and the same deity is called.

Ishtar exists under one form or another in every religion. She is called Ashtorat in the Old Testament. To the Greeks she was known as Aphrodite, and the Romans knew her as Venus, and the Assyrians knew her as Semiramis. To Celtic and Anglo-Saxon witches she was "the queen of heaven," or simply "the Mother Goddess." Even Christianity has taken some of her aspects in creating the image of the Madonna.

A female deity is very necessary for mankind to understand itself, because the female goddess stands at the beginning of life itself. Dr. Paul M. Vest in an article called "Ishtar, Goddess of Love," says that "in the days of Ishtar, veneration of sexual phenomena was customary. It was mankind's primal response to the great force which is the direct source of all life. Consequently, adoration of sex and sex symbols was common to many early religions. And broadly speaking, the goddess Ishtar personified sex, fertility, and the female reproductive life force."

In Feraferia the mechanics of sex are not stressed, but, rather, the spiritual unfolding that leads to love and being in tune with nature. At one point, Adams was interested in the American nudist movement, but later discovered that the motivations of his mystic involvement differed greatly from the health aspects of nudism as it is generally known today. Whereas the shedding of clothes and playing in the sun seemed to be the main objectives of traditional nudism, Adams considers this only the first step in the right direction. Once the outer garments have been stripped off, it is necessary to attune the inner man to nature. Walking around a few hours without clothes and then returning to civilization and life as usual is not enough. Only when we readjust our thinking and feeling completely to total naturalness, whether we wear clothes or not, do we hold out hope that our civilization can still be saved from self-destruction.

"The Feraferian vision includes new inspirations and new combinations from the most ancient well-springs of the goddess. Innovations there are, but always in continuity with those ancient sources," Fred Adams explains. "You will find in the Feraferian vision no slavish archaeological reconstructions, because the new paganism must accommodate all the new developments in human knowledge and awareness that have occurred since the old paganism quite deservedly lost its congregations and crumbled to ruin."

Fred Adams is a marvelously gifted painter. His interpretations of the mystery gods of ancient Greece rank favorably with some of the classical originals. Adams calls his incantations for the days of the week "enchantments." The idea is not to beseech the goddess or to threaten her in order to force her to perform what is wanted, but rather to entice her, enchant her with charm, charisma, expressions of love and devotion. In other words, a positive approach to the goddess, all the way. Feraferia's periodical, *Korythalia,* contains some of his poetry.

The following is an example of what you might read in this publication:

Beginning with Saturday, the day sacred to Saturn, the enchantments differ for each day of the week. These are not specific incantations but are rather like morning prayers in the Christian religion. In a way they are requests for guidance and the blessings of the day.

Ourania-Aphaia-Pheraia-Despoina,
I dedicate this day to thee and to thine own land—
sky—love-body of deep heaven,
All stars, all grounds and matrices of existence,
The geosphere, polar ice caps, tundra, and alpine fell.

Blessed be thy faerie realms. They will grow in wilderness and love, even as they suffuse my presence with joy and wilderness wisdom. Grant all wildlings in these realms thrive, find fulfillment and rebirth. I bestow my genius and love upon these realms and all their wildlings. May the wild realms of Ourania, black goddess of stars, bestow upon me their genius for mystery, that divine ground-essence, immanence, transcendence, lasting value, eternity, wholeness, plurality, magistery, magnanimity, merging field cohesion, peace, cosmic completion, ultimate consummations. May I dance in the endless wedding procession of Ourania and Kronos, of alpine peaks and tone forests, as it winds through mazes of starlight in the nuptial night of the nameless bride! Evoekore! Evoekoros! Awiya!

According to Mr. Adams, the proper time for cosmic communion is Saturday, the Sabbath, and the night of Ourania, at nine P.M. This is also the time for meditation, and, of course, meeting of covens. The second day of the week, Sunday, is sacred to Helois, the sun god. Monday is sacred to Artemis, and it is the third day of the week in the pagan calendar. Tuesday, the fourth day, belongs to Hermes-Pan, and Wednesday is sacred to Aphrodite. Thursday belongs to Ares, the god of war; Friday is dedicated to Kronos-Zeus-Godfather.

Also, according to Mr. Adams, the night of Diana is the proper time for such psychic enterprises as astral projection, scrying, and magic. Nine P.M. is the proper hour for the circle of members of a coven to lie in star formation on the ground, heads together at the center, arms loosely touching all around. It is also a good time to trance-dance for specific magical purposes.

"The very backbone of the pagan movement is the calendar," Fred Adams explains. But this does not mean the calendar in the conventional sense, but rather living completely in tune with natural rhythm of life, doing whatever is appropriate at any given moment of the calendar, and avoiding that which is contrary to its position.

Feraferia celebrates a number of festivals during the calendar year. The beginning of the year, or vernal equinox, falls on March 21. It is called Ostara, and in the sacred circle it represents the east. Ostara celebrates the awakening in nature, the beginning of the new year, the end of winter. It is a joyous occasion and generally involves outdoor festivities.

Next comes May Day, or Beltane. However, in Wicca this holiday is marked on May Eve, April 30. Beltane is described as "the festival of full flowering; sex crowns the holy nakedness of blossoming flesh. By sex the two are divided only to be molded closer in bliss."

The summer solstice, or midsummer, is celebrated on June 21. This represents the longest day of the year and the full union in nature of all that is alive, "both in each," according to the Feraferian calendar.

August 1 is called Lamas, or sometimes Lugnasad. This festival represents the height of summer fertility, the culmination of all that man has strived for during winter and spring.

The autumnal equinox, on September 23, is a celebration of homecoming. It represents the harvesting of fruit, both in the field and in human experience.

November 1 is the day of Samhain, also called All Souls' Day and in Wicca celebrated the night before as Hallowe'en. Far from being a jolly occasion filled with levity, it is a thought-provoking day of reflection at the beginning of winter. In Wicca the reign of the horned god begins while the Mother Goddess rests. In Feraferia this is a time when new members may be initiated into the coven or when the "dread doors between worlds swing open." It is a time, then, for listening to the voices of the occult, both within and without.

On December 21, a day of thanksgiving is celebrated. It is also called a day of repose, since it signifies the return of the elements into the soil, when nature rests in preparation for the spring to come. The following day, December 22, is the day of Yule, or winter solstice. This is a celebration of first awakening, since at this point the sun turns north again, and heralds the coming of distant spring. Yule, therefore, is a joyous celebration even though nature still sleeps.

February 10 is the festival of Olmelc, known as Candlemas. This festival of the lights is called Brigid's Day in some covens because the prettiest member of the coven is selected to perform the ritual of the eternal bride.

Finally, on March 21, the vernal equinox, the magic circle is completed and the new year begins.

Today when we speak of group sex, involvement, and sensitivity training, that which was taboo not so long ago has become experimental, and what is experimental today may very well be the norm among some of tomorrow's advanced societies. In many ways, Feraferia's theories are only a little ahead of current views. Adams states, "There is a decided connection between the anti-pagan waste of man's erotic potential and his laying waste of earth's ecological potential," meaning that frustrated people like to destroy what they cannot possess, while happy people prefer to see a happy world around them. "The fullest expression of kindness depends on the fullest experience of sensual grace. Love clusters of committed persons who constitute themselves experimental families will have the function of developing communal living and sexuality within the paradisal context."

Practically speaking, Feraferia believes that physical contact between the skin of man and the natural environment, between flesh and plant, in activities they call "play-love-work" and which includes sports, playfulness, and lovemaking, can actually work to the advantage of both. Man derives strength and revitalization from coming into contact with unspoiled wilderness, nature, growing things, plants and trees. And they feel that nature, by being touched directly by living bodies, obtains new eneriges with which to purify itself and to ensure its continued growth.

For example, this conviction is expressed in a ritual best undertaken on Beltane, or May Day, for the benefit of improving the landscape. "Some individuals or groups may enchant within actual grass environments at these times. If you make love *for* the grasses *in* the grasses, then you follow the most ancient and venerable precedents and newly initiate the most progressive psycho-religious processes of earth-self integration."

The ritual then continues:

> The foreplay may be enjoyed as dance, ranging far and wide over the swards of Ares. As lovers caress each other on the move, clasp and unclasp while running and rolling through grass-scapes, they at the same time caress, rub, pummel, and exchange blades and tufts of grass between them. Their being becomes saturated with grassiness until love longing is the very surge of chlorophyll. On the green wave of orgasm, they flow together into the landscape. Land and sky become their fused body of love, their unified land-sky-love-body.

Let us suppose we wanted to construct a "henge" to worship Kore, the magic maiden. The spot chosen should be physically beautiful and have a certain sense of what Fred Adams calls "aliveness."

First, one must drive a stake into the center of the chosen area and mark off a circle at least ten feet in diameter. The circle may be larger, if that is possible. Around the circle one must dig a shallow ditch about eight inches wide and deep, which represents the "round river of the sacred year." This is the preliminary step. On the first clear, moonless night, one must go out into the garden or backyard and drive a stake into the soil near the inside edge of the shallow ditch representing the round river. The spot is a point where a line drawn from the center of the circle crosses the ditch and thereby seems to connect to Polaris, better known as the North Star.

The following day, a line must be drawn from the Yule point, which is the spot one has marked the previous night, through the center, and on to the mid-summer point, or south on the other side. There another stake is to be driven into the ground. In similar manner, the east and west points are marked off, either with chains or ropes or tapes, and stakes driven into the soil at the east and west points. Then the four points midway between the cardinal points are marked off in such a way that all eight points by the edge of the round river are an equal distance from one another. Stone or wooden markers called *menhirs* are then placed on these eight spots and in the center.

Of course, that is only the beginning. Assuming that one has created one's own henge to worship in the pagan manner and is ready to use it, there is still the matter of a proper incantation. How does one approach the sacred precinct for the first time? Through its poetic high priest, Feraferia suggests the following prayer:

> We stand before the temple of Great Nature, mandala of the sacred year, mandala of the sacred self, psycho-cosmic tuning dial of an eternal metamorphosis through perennial sacrament. Hail, Great Goddess. Evoe Kore! Hearken to the mythologos of the sacred year. We worship the divine lovers, eternal goddess of nature and containment and perennial god of purpose and penetration. Their union is the pattern of creation. They are the protogenesis of all things. Their celestial thrones are moon and sun. Their love ground of the year is the everlasting religion of nature, the inspired dance of the seasons. Evoe Kore! Evoe Kouros! Awiya!

Naturally, Feraferia is not for *everyone;* not everyone should think that Feraferia is for him or that he will be accepted for membership. All ancient cults were selective in their admission of new members. This must be so to preserve the power, integrity, and purpose of the cult. Thinning the blood makes it weaker; spreading the sacred truths too far afield lessens their impact where they are most needed.

I have discovered that the Church of the Eternal

Source used to be housed in what was once the coven-sted of Sarah Cunningham's Wicca congregation. The leaders of this Egyptian congregation explain:

> The Egyptian religion is a religion of joy and light, of festivals and celebrations, because the universe is basically a very happy place. It is a religion of freedom and individual choice, where all the gods are available at all times, each in its sphere, each as required with its own special powers, to serve each individual at each moment precisely as required and, when desired, to lead the individual to that vision of unity and completion which is the highest divine grace. It is a religion of reality where the gods stand clearly visible to man and where their power can be felt. It is a religion of passions, of the deepest emotions, of love, compassion, excitement, of inspiration and of exhilaration. Most important it is a religion which works, which brings prosperity and happiness to the individual and his society.

This second Mediterranean cult in modern America is also located in California. The Church of the Eternal Source observes its own formalities as a religious group. There are nine degrees of initiate in this congregation, from the lowly aspirant, brother or sister, neophyte, zelator, novitiate, proselyte, initiate, priest, to the ninth and highest, the high priest. On the first Wednesday of each month there is a ritual of Thoth, presided over by Don Harris. On the second Wednesday of each month Jimmy Kemble performs the ritual of Osiris. The third Wednesday is dedicated to the gods in general while the fourth Wednesday belongs to Horus. The latter is presided over by Harold Moss. The calendar of the church even lists a fifth Wednesday, apparently during months when there are five Wednesdays in a given thirty-one-day period. The latter belongs to all the gods together. The church provides the services of its priesthood for personal counseling, counseling through divinations, marriages, funerals, blessings of infants, and other sundries ordinarily performed by the Servants of God. The congregation is growing; in July 1971 a birthday party for the goddess Isis was attended by forty-three people from as far away as San Diego, and the costumes, according to eyewitness reports, were truly magnificent.

I learned that the calendar of celebrations is filled with activities. Undoubtedly, the members' artistic creativity and imagination are stimulated by their involvement with this group. Harold Moss and his associates are indeed learned people, so a member is likely to absorb much information on Egyptian history and comparative religion. Yoga, meditation, and chanting are part of the curriculum. The use of tarot cards, astrology, the *I Ching,* even crystal gazing and the use of the pendulum are taught and practiced in this congregation. The production of art works is encouraged. The leaders of the group encourage exploring the wilderness and arrange hiking and camping trips. "The gods dance in wilderness. It is out of wilderness we emerged." By 1973 the Church of the Eternal Source had established a new branch at New Bedford, Massachusetts.

The Order of Osirus (from "Osiris") is a kind of Egyptian witchcraft organization. The order's headquarters is at Box 654, Kearny, Nebraska, 68847. The letterhead of the organization shows a bucranium, that is, a horned bull, through which a trident is thrust, and the date 1572. The members use colorful witchcraft names and the membership seems to be national. I was supplied with a membership list and here is what I discovered: casting spells and doing good things for people are apparently the main preoccupation of the members. "My desire is to be a good witch. I would like to have a spell to make a baseball and football team win. Also a spell for a better figure, longer hair, and stuff like that," a Pennsylvania member is quoted. The order apparently supplies books and various occult objects to its members. "The articles I ordered are really good and they have helped me greatly. The charms, the hex stones, they all will protect me. I am not bothered with no more trouble. The breaking-spells stone helps me greatly, so no one can do anything to me. God bless you all," a member from Virginia informs headquarters.

Still another kind of Egyptian religion worships only one supreme deity, Aton, instead of a multitude of gods. The Egyptian Church of Chicago, also called the Congregation of Universal Enlightenment, is located at 2551 Halstead Street, Chicago, Illinois 60614. It is under the guidance of "His Excellence, the Arkon Charles Renslow, spiritual head of the Egyptian faith of North and South America." The church does not sell books, or religion for that matter, and does not even pass the hat for donations—a most unchurchly attitude! The Chicago church is primarily the personal expression of its founding father: "May the creator of peace and love dwell in your heart and open your minds to knowledge and truth."

The Sabaeans, also of Chicago, are headed by Frederico de Arechaga. He is about thirty years old and dresses in the most elegant Spanish styles, which is not surprising since he is of Spanish-Basque origin. Mr. de Arechaga speaks perfect English, choosing his words with great care. He makes a living with an occult shop called El Sabarum on North Halstead Street in Chicago. There you can buy all kinds of occult supplies, from candles to jewelry and robes, whether you are a member of his Sabaean society or not. On the counter there are copies of the society's newsletter, called *Janus,* which contains a lunar calendar and sophisticated discussions of witchcraft and of the meanings of gods and goddesses.

In many ways, the Sabaeans follow the astrological and ecological principles held dear by Fred Adams and his Feraferia group in Pasadena. However, Feraferia's traditions are mainly ancient Greek intermingled with some Celtic ritual, while the Sabaeans are a Babylonian cult that has reamined alive through centuries of persecution.

It appears that the term *saba* comes from the Holy Koran. "We have a special philosophy," de Arechaga explained to me. "We relate to the Old Religion, but we do not believe in hero worship. We eliminate competition and the need to identify. Consequently, we do not like to speak of ourselves, but rather of ideas." De Arechaga's mother had been a high priestess in Spain, and pagan traditions are part of his family history. His Sabaean philosophy continues a very ancient tradition that was also the religion of Spain in the megalithic age. This tradition antedates both Christianity and Mohammedanism. De Arechaga explained, "We are identified with the great Mother Goddess. I am all that is, was, and ever shall be. Our god is a divinity with two faces, which relates to the sixty-fourth chapter of the Egyptian Book of the Dead. Because we are yesterday, today, and tomorrow, what purpose would there be in knowing tomorrow if you could not change it today? There is only one reality we believe in, and that is the reality of *now*. Reality is your personal experience. We are not hedonistic. We are henotheistic."

According to Hans Holzer's description of a Venus festival of this group, in *The Witchcraft Report,* it was an experience he'll never forget.

In March of 1973 I took part in a Venus festival the likes of which I haven't seen described in either book, film, or, for that matter, opera. Between the emotionally tinged music of the temple orchestra, the impressive and highly sensual dancing of three young female temple dancers, unencumbered by too much clothing, the genuine upsurge of joy amongst the congregation honoring the love goddess through dancing and singing, I was swept along by the tide of the eternal life force expressing itself in these quarters. White columns decorated with wreaths, a life-size statue of Ishtar, the Astaroth of the Old Testament, in back of the main altar, incense rising from the offering table, and flaming candelabras flanking the goddess created an indelible imprint in me. The Venus festival was not an open one but newly created initiates were permitted to be present. As with earlier visits to the temple of El Saba, I was given a place of honor due to my past initiations. Following the ritual, the congregation shared a meal composed of fruit, sea food, and meat in true Pagan fashion: with their hands.

De Arechaga pointed out the striking parallels existing between the Sumerian Pagan rituals and some of the Mexican and Central American heritage. It is his conviction that the people of Central America worshipped in an "old religion of their own," perhaps of common origin with the Mediterranean Pagan religion. "The Mexicans are a comparatively recent addition to monotheism," the spiritual leader of the Sabaeans explained, "but the Aztecs did not, in fact, really convert. They are not only genuine American Pagans but they are still practicing today and their rites relate a great deal to the Indians of North America."

Ancient beliefs vie with ancient relics in our museums for the attention of the curious. But if it strikes you as strange that the gods of ancient Egypt, Greece, and Rome should be resurrected by worshipers in the 1970s in sophisticated America, stop for a moment and think: Isn't Christianity based upon the philosophy and life of a man who lived in ancient Judaea two thousand years ago? Doesn't much of the Far East look to a deified prophet who trod the earth six hundred years before the Christian era? What is time to the gods? Spiritual truth is timeless.

9

Love Potions, Herbs, and Scents

What is meant by love? As used by Latin writers, the word has a range of meanings, from that of sexual relation between insects and animals up to the highest form of religious emotion, called the love of God. All through the ages people have tried to define it. Love is a subject that knows no bounds.

The love charms in existence today are just as boundless in numbers and kinds. Some are quaint, some crude, and a few quite beautiful, but all are potentially effective. Their merit lies not so much in the procedures they recommend as in the effect they have in the mind of whoever uses them. Love charms concentrate the performer's attention on the person of his choice, in whose mind a reciprocal interest is telepathically aroused. The charm then "draws down" the force needed to accomplish the intention behind it.

The philtre, or love potion, is frequently mentioned in medieval literature. The name is applied to a liquid composed of wine as a base, with the addition of expertly mixed herbs or drugs to give it the property of inspiring in the man or woman who drinks it irresistible love for some specified person. In heroic epics and plays, it is a powerful dramatic motive force, easy to set to work and of the greatest utility in "difficult" situations.

In the romance of Tristan and Iseult, a philtre intended by Iseult's mother for King Mark is drunk by Iseult and Tristan together, and it fills them with the passion that was to be fatal to them in the end. Richard Wagner, in the *Götterdämmerung,* made use of another philtre to turn Siegfried from Brynhilde and fire him with love for Gutrune, although this incident is not mentioned in the Scandinavian sagas from which he drew the elements of his musical tragedy.

I read one recipe in Emile Grillot de Givry's work, which sounds especially complicated:

> To make onself beloved there shall be taken, to wit, the heart of a dove, the liver of a sparrow, the womb of a swallow, the kidney of a hare, and they shall be reduced to impalpable powder. Then the person who shall compound the philtre shall add an equal part of his own blood, dried and in the same way powdered. If the person whom it is desired to draw into love is caused to swallow this powder in a dose of 2 or 3 drachms, marvelous success will follow.

To differentiate—spells rely solely on mental powers and energy flows, whereas the philtre is a purely chemical weapon. Combined with the spell, it may work, but one cannot be sure whether it is the philtre that does the trick or the spell!

A "love potion" may use any drug that lowers the reasoning powers of a person—provided that the other party is there when the drug takes effect. The immediate presence of the petitioner is not necessary to get results when certain hallucinogenic plant extracts lasting a day or two are used in the concoction. But there are no long-range philtres that can still influence a person weeks or months after it has been absorbed into the bloodstream. That much is pure fiction.

A practitioner of magic often tells the one desiring the philtre to speak a certain phrase while giving the potion to the prospective "victim," but this is more a mental support for the purpose of positive suggestion than an actual aid to the philtre itself.

The verbalization can take many forms, such as this one: "May this potion enter ————'s body and soul as my thoughts enter his/her mind. May it bring him/her to me with all dispatch." Magic, working with spells, incantations, and other verbal tools, is pretty much in the same position as its more "legitimate" cousin, religion. Does it work? Do mere words cause action?

Of course, love spells did not always take the form

of a liquid. Since it was often difficult to make the person desired drink the potion, easier methods were devised, such as the use of talismans. The use of the philtre proper was abandoned to some extent by the eighteenth century. I discovered an ancient prescription for a love potion in De Givry's book. It is taken from an eighteenth-century manuscript entitled *Opération des Sept Esprits des Planèts,* and has a subdivision that in English means "Magic Secrets for Making Oneself Beloved." From the manuscript I quote one of the fifty secrets:

> To gain the love of a girl or a woman you must pretend to cast her horoscope—that is to say, when she shall be married—and must make her look right into your eyes. When you are both in the same position, you are to repeat the words: "Kafé, Kasita, non Kafela et Publia Filii Omnibus Suis." These words said, you will command the female and she will obey you in all your desire.

According to authority Paul Huson, the athame (or dagger) is never used in love spells. Many of the lesser love spells make use of philtres and potions for the raising and transmission of magical power; it is the chalice that contains them at their compounding which provides the focus for the invoked force. The chalice is dedicated to certain subtler powers of the unseen, which are considered feminine in relation to the more-violent nature of those invoked in works of, say, wrath and chastisement; the chalice powers are invoked by means of a symbolism somewhat familiar to that of the classical deities of love, such as Venus and Amor. Indeed, the chalice is obviously sexual in its implications of receptive passivity, as opposed to the more thrusting aggressiveness of the wand and the athame.

The place of your work must be sealed off from all intrusion at the correct time of day. The altar table, topped with a triangular cover, should be placed in its usual or central position; one angle always points east. Your cup with one light on either side should stand in the center of the triangle. On the altar there should be a thurible and a box of suitable incense. Then assemble the materials for your philtre, a mortar and pestle and, of course, your workbook in which the spell has been previously written out. Finally, surround the altar triangle with a circle of fresh, sweet-smelling flowers, like freesia, narcissus or lilac, jasmine or carnation.

Having seen to your initial preparations, light the lamps and kindle the incense, chanting as you do such words of consecration as: "In thy name, Habondia, and that of thy Ministers of Love, do I proceed in this work of Love."

A simple spell for lovers has been used for centuries by witches; the Coriander Spell. Pour a small quantity of pure distilled water into the chalice, and count seven coriander seeds into your mortar. Pound these well and strongly summoning an image in your mind's eye of the person or persons the spell is designed to affect, call their names aloud three times, and chant these words, "Warm seed, warm heart, let them never be apart." Then cast the powder into the chalice, imagining as you do that the full force of your desire enters it also. See it as a flame descending on the surface of the liquid. Complete the spell with the words, "So mote it be!" and draw the seal of the triple cross in the air above the cup with your right forefinger. Leave the herb to steep for about twelve hours, then strain the philtre through fine muslin or cheesecloth and introduce it secretly into the food or drink of the person or persons the spell is desired to affect.

Another useful potion, called Periwinkle, consists of taking dried leaves of periwinkle (Vinca major or minor), Mercury herbs, cinquefoil, vervain, and rose petals. Place them in your mortar and grind them to a fine powder. As you do so, repeat over and over a jingle to declare your intent, such as, "By this act I draw [name] and [name] into a bond of love and desire." Then take two very small pinches of the resultant powder, mix them with the water in the chalice, again charging it with the full force of your crystallized libido, and again seal with the triple cross and the words, "So mote it be." Leave the philtre to steep for twelve hours, strain through fine muslin or cheesecloth, and introduce it secretly into the food or drink of those named in the charm.

Finally, there is another ancient favorite—the True Love Philtre. It is no less effective than the former potions, when properly done, but is less used because one of its main ingredients, mistletoe berries, is abundant only at Christmastime.

The procedure for concocting the True Love Philtre does not vary from that of the Periwinkle spell, save in its ingredients, which are dried seeds or flowers of elecampane, dried vervain leaves, and dried mistletoe berries. Pound and mix with water in the chalice exactly the same way as in the Periwinkle spell.

Of course, witches have been the chief suppliers of love potions and philtres throughout the ages. LaVoisin, in Louis XIV's time, often employed revolting ingredients in his concoctions, like powdered moles with a pinch of the poisonous cantharides, or Spanish fly. This was, and still is, a sure giveaway of the inefficient witch. The bludgeoning effect of drugs is the last resort of the ineffectual spell-binder. Witchcraft is effected by *magical* art, not by chemical means.

For at least five hundred years, witches have also made extensive use of herbs, often for their powerful chemical properties, but equally often for properties not as well known.

During the Stone Age, man began raising plants and animals methodically, after the northern ice caps had melted, transforming the wastes of Europe into temperate forest regions. Between 4000 and 3000 B.C. the discovery of copper and bronze did more to speed civilization than anything else had done. Around 3000 B.C. men took their new tools and weapons and began moving westward through Europe and crossing the ever-widening newly melted polar waters, which now divided the mainland from the British Isles, bringing with them their knowledge of cattle-breeding and wheat farming. At about the same time, the pharaoh Narmer was unifying upper and lower Egypt and founding the first reported pharaonic dynasty. In Mesopotamia, the Sumerians were inventing their cuneiform writing. Herbs were undoubtedly being used. However, it was in the Far East that our first detailed reference to herbs was made, a few hundred years later, in what was an advanced civilization even in those early days. Shen-Nung, the "Red Emperor"—so called because of the "fiery" quality of his personality—used himself as a guinea pig to study the effects of various herbs upon the human constitution. He concluded that the ginseng plant was the king of all herbs and a genuine promoter of longevity, and even today the Chinese think of it as just that. Shen-Nung's own long life seems to have given eloquent support to his observations, for he died at the ripe old age of 123!

In 1500 B.C., the Egyptian pharaoh Thutmose III sent an expedition to Syria in search of new and useful medicinal plants, among other things. Relief of some of the plants it returned with can be seen today carved upon the walls of Thutmose's own temple in Karnak. Among the plants are many recognizable irises, sunflowers, lotuses, pomegranates, and arum lilies, all of them once highly valued botanical medicines. From the books of the Old Testament we know that a large variety of herbs and spices besides these were also raised in ancient Mesopotamia. For example, the prophet Jeremiah alludes to the balm of Gilead, a rare aromatic gum that the historian Josephus tells us was presented as a gift to King Solomon by none other than the Queen of Sheba! The Song of Solomon mentions frankincense, myrrh, camphor, saffron, cinnamon, spikenard, calamus, and aloe—all still considered valuable items in the herbal pharmacopoeia.

Between 500 and 400 B.C. the Greeks made the first serious attempt in the West to systematize their herbal lore in writing. A number of herbalist books began to appear, all of them attributed to the famous physician Hippocrates, the Father of Medicine. They catalog and describe nearly four hundred useful plants. Although their actual authorship is debatable, Hippocrates' name helped to earn them lasting respect through the centuries. Around 400 B.C., the lists were improved upon by a botanist from Euboea, Diocles of Carystus, whose book is now recognized as the first complete Western herbal. Soon after Hippocrates died, the ships of Alexander the Great began to return from the conquest of the East, laden with plunder. Herbs and exotic spices were included among other treasures. Mangrove, cotton, and euphorbium made their appearance in the Western world, along with such now-familiar spices as cinnamon and saffron. Theophrastus of Ephesus, like Alexander a pupil of Aristotle, capitalized on this influx of new Oriental herbal lore in his *History of Plants,* which he wrote about 300 B.C. Besides providing an encyclopedia of useful plants, common and exotic, Theophrastus also revealed tantalizing glimpses of the dark workings of the rhizotomists, a fraternity of herbalists who wove their lore into a semireligious cult and practiced magical rituals strongly reminiscent of those of the Druids, the mysterious oak priests of ancient Britain. The wise physicians of the Arabian Empire were not slow to recognize the value of Dioscorides' monumental work. Neither were those of Byzantium.

Throughout the Middle Ages, most monasteries followed the example of Italy's Monte Cassino and studied herbalism. Dispensing Christian charity, which included healing the sick, was one of their primary duties. Each monastery owned a private herb garden and every library had copies of Apuleius and Dioscorides, now lavishly illustrated in color and gold leaf. Even today, monastery ruins frequently contained old medicinal herbs growing among the weeds.

Paracelsus, a German physician born in 1493, complicated herbalism's evolution as a science with his *Doctrine of Signatures.* In brief, it claimed that every plant was "signed" or associated by a mysterious spiritual bond to a particular disease. The clue to which disease could be found in the shape, scent, color, or even habitat of the herb itself. For example, lungwort (sticta pulmonaria), whose spotted leaves were thought to resemble lungs, remedied bronchial complaints. Euphraisia officianalis, whose flowers hold a resemblance to bright eyes, was considered a good remedy for sore eyes and ophthalmia.

The next great turning point in herbal history was the appearance of John Gerard's *herbal* of 1597. In the same way that Alexander's expedition had benefited early herbalism, Columbus' trip to the Western world did in 1492. Gerard's famous herbal showed Europe hitherto unknown plants from "The New Land called America" among which were the potato, the tomato (called by him the Apple of Love), and tobacco.

In 1653, Nicholas Culpeper, the herbalist, successfully combined astrology with herbalism after the manner of the ancients in his famous book, "Complete Herbal." Since astrology was quite popular in Culpeper's day, he had a ready-made audience. However, academic interest in herbalism all but died with the advent of the eighteenth and nineteenth centuries, although in rural districts of Britain, Continental Europe, and the United States herbal medicine continued to be popular and useful. *American Medicinal Plants,* written by C. F. Millspaugh in 1887, is still a classic in the field. This herbal supplemented and enlarged the European herbal information with a wealth of native American plants.

During the twentieth century, official interest in herbs revived in a dramatic and quite unforeseen mannner, strangely enough due to the outbreak of the two world wars. Interest in herbs has grown steadily over the past four years. During the last decade, it has, of course, received a considerable boost from books such as Aldous Huxley's *Doors of Perception* and the interest they have sparked in botanical psychoactive agents such as cannabis and peyote. But the wave of interest in plants and herbs that is sweeping the Western world is far more general, and cannot be said to be limited to those who are simply exploring the plant world for its potential psychoactive properties.

Paul Huson gives practical samples of herbs useful in cures, herbs used by witches for centuries without benefit of medical training, but with good results.

blood purifiers: agrimony, burdock root, yarrow.
burns: balm of Gilead, comfrey, elder, yarrow.
colds and fevers: agrimony, angelica root, balm, boneset, camomile, catnip, elder flowers, fenugreek, feverfew, horehound, hissop, pennyroyal, peppermint, sage, spearmint, thyme, verbena, wormwood, yarrow.

congestion: coltsfoot, comfrey root, horehound, mullein.

constipation: butternut root, dandelion, cascara sagrada, senna.

coughs: agrimony, angelica root, coltsfoot, comfrey, elecampane, feverfew, garlic, horehound, hissop, marshmallow, menil leaves, red clover tops, speedwell, thyme, vervain, yerba santa.

cuts and abrasions: burnet, cranesbill, garlic, marigold, marshmallow, meadowsweet, plantain, southernwood, thyme, valarian, woodruff.

diarrhea: borage, cinquefoil, comfrey, marjoram, marshmallow, nettle leaves, plantain.

emmenagogues: blue chosh, motherwort, parsley seed, pennyroyal, rue, sage, southernwood, tansy, wintergreen leaves.

flatulence: angelica root, bergamot, catnip, marjoram, pennyroyal.

headache: basil, camomile, lavender, rosemary, thyme, wood betony.

hemmorrhage: red rose buds.

hiccups: dill, fennel, juniper berry, spearmint.

indigestion: camomile, dill, garlic, marjoram, pennyroyal, peppermint, savory, spearmint, thyme, verbena, woodruff.

kidney action, to promote: angelica root, borage, dandelion, garlic, fennel, feverfew, meadowsweet, parsley root and leaves.

mouthwash and gargle: agrimony, cinquefoil, fenugreek, goldenrod, raspberry leaves, sage, thyme.

nausea: basil, burgamot, golden seal, marjoram, pennyroyal, peppermint, spearmint.

perspiration, to promote: angelica root, balm, burnet, camomile, catnip, elder flowers, garlic, hissop, lime (linden) flowers, pennyroyal, thyme, yarrow.

poultices: comfrey root, garlic, marshmallow, plantain, sage, thyme.

rheumatism: angelica root, basil, butmien, hissop.

sedatives: bugle weed, camomile, catnip, hops, lady's slipper (use one-half teaspoon herb to one cup boiling water), lime or linden flowers, motherwort, mullein, primrose, scullcap, malarian, verbena.

spots and pimples: agrimony, speedwell.

sprains: comfrey root, marshmallow, sage, wormwood.

stimulants: anise seeds, cinnamon, cloves, coffee beans, elecampane, feverfew, garlic, ginger root, goldenrod, hawthorn, hissop, lavender, lovage, marigold, marjoram, pennyroyal, peppermint, rosemary, rue, sage, savory, southernwood, spearmint, tea, vervain, woodruff, wormwood, yarrow, yerba maté.

stomach cramps: bergamot, burdot leaves, camomile, colt's foot, comfrey root, fenugreek, marshmallow, meadowsweet, peppermint, sage, thyme.

teething trouble: clove, peppermint, yarrow.

tonic, body-building: alfalfa.

tonics: agrimony, buckbean, burnet, catnip, centaury, camomile, coltsfoot, dandelion, feverfew, lovage, marjoram, meadowsweet, motherwort, nettle leaves, rosemary, sage, sarsaparilla, sassafras, southernwood, thyme, vervain, wormwood.

vertigo: primrose.

I discovered that "psychic perfumes" are one of the specialties of the learned witch Sara Cunningham, who lives and teaches witchcraft in Boulder, Colorado. Since ancient times there have been many legends regarding the vibratory power of exotic fragrances. There are special blends for love, peace, prosperity, health, meditation, magnetism, prayer, etc., which come down to us from antiquity. While one cannot make any claims of supernatural forces for these fragrances, one cannot lightly dismiss the beliefs of centuries. Oils are blended by Sara in strict accordance with the ancient formulas, it seems. No compromise is made in the ingredients, and there are no substitutes or synthetic additives. Essential oils are preferred by the majority, due to the fact that the fragrance lasts far longer than that of perfumes or colognes, nor do they evaporate, since no alcohol or synthetic bases are used in these oils, Sara explains.

Here are some of the scents possessed of magical qualities, according to Sara Cunningham:

anointing oil: a blend of sacred oils for blessing candles, altar equipment.

bergamot: said to protect one from misfortune and negativity.

cypress: said to bring good fortune and blessings. It is one of the oils sacred to the Zoroastrians.

frankincense: one of the sacred oils, it is used on altar equipment, candles, and worn on the body. Said to bring great blessings and have high spiritual vibration.

heliotrope: said to have highly spiritual vibrations; used in psychic work.

hyacinth: said to be very relaxing; used to promote peaceful sleep or deep meditation.

isis: one of the sacred scents of the Egyptian great goddess, Isis.

jasmine: one of the sacred oils of the great goddess and of the Virgin Mary.

lavendar: said to promote peace and purify the atmosphere. It is also said to possess healing vibrations.

lilac: used as an aid to far memory and the recalling of past incarnations.

lotus: sacred to the Great Mother. It is said to bring blessings and promote peace and health.

magnet oil: used to draw and magnetize.

musk: sacred to the Great Goddess, it is said to aid the willpower and magnetize the personality.

myrrh: another of the sacred oils, it has a very high spiritual effect.

narcissus: said to possess healing vibrations.

petule: said to promote peace and ward off evil.

red rose: said to promote peace, love, and affection.

rosemary: wards off evil and is said to be a powerful antidote to Black Magic.

sandalwood: said to possess highly spiritual vibrations and to promote healing.

vervain: said to aid in material matters, and to stimulate creativity.

violet: said to have strong healing vibrations, promote peace, and remove negative influences.

Janus: sacred to the forest god, strictly a man's vibration.

moon mist: said to possess very high psychic vibrations, excellent for all serious occultists.

Star Fire: said to bring one under the influence of the Astral Teachers.

Satyr: highly volatile on the sensual plane, said to vibrate on a highly sexual key, not to be worn by the timid.

Danu: sacred to the Great Goddess in her forest aspect, said to bring blessings and protection.

Circe: the favorite scent of the legendary sorceress, said to attract the opposite sex.

Bacchus: sacred to the god of wine and pleasure, this oil is for the fun-loving swingers only.

Wicca: one of the sacred anointing oils of the craft, said to invoke the blessings of the god and goddess.

Incenses are equally potent tools of witchcraft. Sara Cunningham supplies occultists and witches with the required aromatics, such as these:

Kyphi: this is the same incense that was used in the ancient Egyptian temples in 2000 B.C. It is a rare blend of resins, herbs, and honey, according to a recipe taken from an ancient papyrus. The vibrations of this unique incense are on the highest spiritual plane and it is excellent for both meditation and ritual use.

Magus: an unusual blend of herbs, resins, and spices that is suitable for all religious and magical rituals.

Evocation: an unusual blend of herbs suitable for any ritual where visualization or manifestation is required. This incense has a very strong vibratory rate.

Isis: sacred to the goddess Isis, said to bring blessings and protection, excellent for use in all rituals where the influence of the Great Goddess is required.

10
The Kabala, Alchemy, and The Hermetic Orders

Kabala means "tradition," i.e., the tradition of things divine. Jewish mysticism is centuries old; it has exerted profound influence on those Jews who were eager to learn the deeper meanings of traditional forms and concepts of Judaism. Documents produced by the Kabalists date as far back as the Middle Ages. However, the main literary work of this movement was the Zohar, or "Book of Splendor." Even today certain Jewish communities revere this work as a sacred text of unquestionable value. The Kabalists had attempted to penetrate and even to describe the mystery of the world as a reflection of the mysteries of divine life. The images into which their experience had crystallized were deeply involved with the historical experience of the Jewish people, which by the nineteenth century seemed to have lost its relevance. At the heart of this reality lay a great image of rebirth, the myth of exile and redemption, which assumed vast dimensions with the Kabalists and accounts for their prolonged historical influence.

When the first Kabalists appeared in Jewish history, in Languedoc at the end of the twelfth century, they did not claim to have spoken directly with God. They took a compromise position. On one hand, they wished to communicate something that obviously had not come to them through the traditional and generally accepted channels. But on the other hand, as Orthodox Jews, they could not claim for their own mystical experience the same rank as that for the revelation underlying the religious authority of Judaism. In rabbinical Judaism, from which the Kabalistic mysticism developed, a number of different revelations were recognized as authentic and each in its own way authoritative, namely, the revelations of Moses, of the prophets, of the Holy Spirit (which spoke through the authors of the Psalms and other parts of the Bible), of the receivers of the "heavenly voice" (*bathkol,* believed to have been audible in the Talmudic era), and finally the "revelation of the prophet Elijah." Each of these stages represents a lesser degree of authority than the stage preceding it. This is why the Kabalists claimed only the modest rank of receivers of a revelation of the prophet Elijah. In this connection it should be remembered that in such experience the auditive factor was most important and the visual factor only secondary, since most importantly, no doubt under the influence of the mystical theory of prophecy referred to above, the Jewish mystics accorded far more importance to the *hearing* of a voice than to visions of light.

All great institutional religions have frowned upon the unlearned mystic who, fired by the intensity of his experience, believes he can bypass the traditional and approved channels of religious life. These lay mystics generally had little information on theology and came into conflict with the established authorities. Regardless of their specific content, all manuals of mysticism written from the standpoint of traditional authority illustrate this point. The Jewish authorities, for example, tried to avoid conflicts by restricting the right to engage in mystical practice and speculation to *fully trained* Talmudic scholars. All Kabalistic manuals contain Maimonides' warning: "No one is worthy to enter paradise [the realm of mysticism] who has not first taken his fill of bread and meat," i.e., the common fare of the sober rabbinical learning.

Through the esoteric tradition of the Kabala, highly ramified mystical tendencies in Judaism developed. The Kabala was not, as it is still sometimes supposed, a unified system of mystical and specifically theosophical thinking. There is no such thing as *"the* doctrine of the Kabalists." Instead, we find diversified and often contradictory sets of motivations, crystallized into very different systems or quasisystems. Fed by currents emanating from the Orient, Kabalism first came to light in those parts of southern France where among non-Jews the Catharist, or Neo-Manichaean, movement was at its height. In thirteenth-century Spain it quickly attained its fullest development, culminating in the pseudo-epigraphic Zohar of Rabbi Moses de Leon, which became a kind of Bible to the Kabalists and for centuries enjoyed an unquestioned position as a sacred and authoritative text. Then in sixteenth-century Palestine, Kabalism was revived and became a central historical and spiritual current in Judaism; for it supplied an answer to the question of the meaning of exile, a question that had taken on a new urgency with the catastrophe of the expulsion of the Jews from Spain in 1492. Fired with Messianic fervor in the seventeenth century, Kabalism became an explosive force in the great Messianic movement centering around Sabbatai Zebi, which even in its collapse provoked a mystical heresy, a heretical Kabala, whose impulses and developments, paradoxically enough, played a significant part—long overlooked and becoming clear to us only today—in the rise of a modern Judaism.

Thus at the heart of the Kabala we have a myth of the one God as a conjunction of all the primordial powers of being and the myth of the Torah as an infinite symbol, in which all images and all names point to a process in which God communicates Himself.

In the thinking of the Jewish mystics, this resurgence of mythical conceptions provided a bond with certain impulses in popular faith, fundamental impulses such as the simple man's fear of life and death, to which Jewish philosophy had no satisfactory response. The mythical character of Kabalistic "theology" mentioned in 1687 by Carpzow, the Protestant theologian, is most clearly manifested in the doctrine of the *sefiroth,* the potencies and modes of action of the living God. In the *Book of Creation,* where the term originates, it means the ten archetypal numbers (from *safar* meaning, to count) taken as the fundamental powers of all being. In this early work, each sefira is not correlated with a vast number of symbols relating it to other archetypal images to form a special structure. This step was first taken by the *Bahir* and the medieval theosophy of the Kabala, which renewed the spiritual and intellectual interpretation of the scriptures concerning the world of aeons and going far beyond them. The totality of these potencies, united in the fundamental *dekas,* forms the world of the *sefiroth,* of the unfolding divine unity that embraces the archetypes of all being. This world, it is emphasized, is a world of divine being, but it overflows without interruption or new beginning into the secret and visible worlds of creation. In the Kabalistic view, this process, which turns outward in creation, is nothing other than the esoteric aspect of a process that takes place in God himself. Nowhere in this cosmogonic myth, which is continued at great length, is there any further mention of *nothing.*

The aura of light, an entirely different aspect, then replaces and surrounds *en-sof,* the infinite, beginningless and uncreated. When, as it does in other passages, the *Zohar* speaks expressly of such a nothing, it is always taken as God's innermost mode of being, which becomes creative in the emanation of the *sefiroth.* "Nothing" in itself is the first and highest of the *sefiroth.* These symbols are enormously rich in mythical implications. But nowhere is the mythical content more evident than in the symbolism that identifies this god of the *sefiroth* with man in his purest form, *Adam Kadmon,* Primordial Man. Here the god, who can be apprehended by man, is himself the First Man. The mythical nature of these conceptions is most clearly exemplified by the distinction between the masculine and feminine, begetting and receiving, potencies in God. This mythical element recurs, with rising intensity, in several pairs of *sefiroth,* and is expressed most forcefully in the symbolism of the last two. The ninth *sefirah, yesod,* is the male potency, described with phallic symbolism, the "foundation" of all life, which consummates the holy union of male and female powers.

The Kabalists stress the interrelation of all worlds and levels of being in their systems. Everything is connected with everything else, and this interpenetration of all things is governed by exact though unfathomable laws. Nothing is without its infinite depth, and from every point this infinite depth can be contemplated. The unity between above and below, the achievement that the *Zohar* designates over and over again as the purpose of the ritual, must accordingly be understood from several aspects. The creation of unity is a mystical action in the depths of the Godhead, because it stimulates the creative power; but at the same time it is in every sense a mythical action, because it unites heaven and earth, the heights and depths of the cosmos.

Certain fundamental concepts that recur in many variants govern the attitude of the Kabala torch ritual. In its role of representation and excitation, the ritual is expected, above all, to accomplish the following:

1. Harmony between the rigid powers of judgment and the flowing powers of mercy.

2. Sacred marriage of the masculine and feminine.

3. Redemption of the *Shekhinah* (community) from its entanglement with the "other side."

4. Defense against, or mastery over, the powers of the "other side."

Many of the Kabalistic rites were strictly esoteric in character, and could only be performed by groups of initiates. In the oldest literature we find descriptions of rites that appear to be special initiations. An example of this kind of initiation is described by Eleazar of Worms (circa 1200):

The name is transmitted only to the reserved—this word can also be translated as "the initiate"—who are not prone to anger, who are humble and God-fearing, and carry out the commandments of their Creator. And it is transmitted only over water. Before the master teaches it to his pupil, they must both immerse themselves and bathe in 40 measures of flowing water, then put on white garments and fast on the day of instruction. Then both must stand up to their ankles in the water, and the master must say a prayer ending with the words: "The voice of God is over the waters! Praised be Thou, O Lord, who revealest Thy secret to those who fear Thee, He who knoweth the mysteries." Then both must turn their eyes toward the water and recite verses from the Psalms, praising God over the waters.

111

At this time the master evidently transmits the one among the secret names of God that the adept is permitted to hear, whereupon they return together to the schoolhouse or synagogue, where they recite a prayer of thanksgiving over a vessel full of water.

Another theurgic ritual comes to us from the same school. I discovered that there are manuscripts in the British Museum, "Book of the Putting On and Fashioning of the Mantle of Righteousness," which shows how names can be literally "put on": first cut a kind of poncho from deerskin parchment. This sleeveless garment with connecting hat is modeled after the high priest's ephod. Then the secret names of God are inscribed on this magic garment. After that the adept must fast for seven days, touch nothing unclean, eat nothing of animal origin, neither eggs nor fish, but only beans, peas, and the like. At the end of seven days he must go at night to the water and call out the name—evidently the name written on the garment—over the water. If he sees a green form in the air above the water it means he is not yet clean and must cleanse himself for another seven days, this time while doing alms and acts of charity. "And pray to your Creator that you will not be shamed once again. And if you see the form in bright red over the water, know that you are inwardly clean and fit to put on the Name. Then go into the water up to your loins and put on the venerable and terrible Name in the water." The ritual is thought to give the adept irresistible strength. He is advised, while "putting on the Name," to invoke the angels associated with it. They appear before him, but all he sees is a moving wisp of smoke. This magic significance of water as the only appropriate medium for such initiation—a conception widespread among non-Jews, e.g., baptism—does not occur in Talmudic literature or in any other Jewish traditions.

The oldest instructions for making a *golem,* or artificial man, must be regarded as a theurgic ritual, in which the adept becomes aware of wielding a certain creative power. According to Talmudic tradition, demons are spirits made in the Friday evening twilight, who, because the Sabbath has intervened, have received no bodies. From this, later authorities drew the inference (perhaps implicit in Talmudic sources) that the demons have been looking for bodies ever since, and that is why they attach themselves to men. This entered into combination with another idea. After the murder of Abel by his brother, Adam decided to have no further dealings with his wife. Thereupon female demons, succubi, came to him and conceived by him; from this union, in which Adam's generative power was misused and misdirected, stem a variety of demons. Abuse of a man's generative powers was held to be a destructive act, through which not the holy but the "other side" obtains progeny. A cult of extreme purity led to the view that every act of impurity, whether conscious or unconscious, engenders demons.

Perhaps even more mysterious, and just as often misunderstood, is the ancient art of alchemy. Just as the Kabala assumes a deeper, inner significance to everything that exists, so alchemy searches for the secret *behind* everything in the world, using the symbolism of gold only in a transcendental way, not as the ultimate goal of the alchemist. In questioning people about alchemy, I found that every one of them thought it was the art of making artificial gold. I researched the subject, and eventually began to understand how easy it is to misinterpret the outer activities of the alchemist, if one does not understand also the underlying purpose and meaning.

Ever since gold was dug out of Egypt's soil in the days of the pharaohs, it has been a mysterious substance. The Egyptians thought it was the sun brought down to earth, and therefore holy. The pharaohs laid claim to all the gold, for they, too, were holy, being born of the sun god. Originally, mining gold was the prerogative of priests. When money came into existence, it was fashioned to the image of the sun and moon, represented by gold and silver, and frequently pictures of the heavenly bodies appeared on coins. Aristotle taught that *all* substances were only variations of gold, the "prime matter," and it was therefore possible to change one into another. Upon this basic concept rests the edifice of alchemy.

In first-century Alexandria, the Greek philosophers came into contact with Judao-Christian theologians and Oriental thinkers, amalgamating their systems in the Gnostic schools. Eventually, Gnosticism was outwardly assimilated with Christianity in order to survive. To the Gnostic, everything is symbolic, and the Bible merely a metaphysical allegory, for the written word contains *deeper* meanings. The heavens are alive with demons and angels, along with Christ and the Holy Trinity.

Gold is both material and human perfection. The only people who could make gold were those whom God felt worthy of the great secret, due to their high degree of purity. From the outset, alchemy served a dual purpose: making gold from baser elements, and making man perfect by eliminating his faults. Material alchemy requires laboratory experiment, fires, elixirs, and chemicals. Spiritual alchemy calls for better understanding of man's destiny through the *inner* meanings of words, colors, sounds, numbers, and symbols— the grasp of magic. Both kinds of alchemy draw upon the secret writings of Hermes Trismegistus. Was he a god? A great teacher who preferred to remain anonymous? The "thrice greatest" Hermes was the mysterious author of the Emerald Tablets, allegedly found in the great pyramid of Cheops.

Thus speaks Hermes Trismegistus:

It is true without doubt and certain: the nether is like the upper and the upper is like the nether, to accomplish the wonders of the one, and even as all things arose from the word of the one, so likewise shall all things by virtue of aggregation be born of the one. His father is the sun, his mother the moon. The wind carried him in its womb, his wet-nurse is the earth. He is the father of all wondrous works in the universe. His Power is complete. It is so transmuted to earth. Separate earth from fire, the fine from the coarse, gently and with great sagacity. It ascends from earth to heaven and down again to earth, to receive the power of the upper and of the nether. Thus you shall call the glorious light of the world your own and all darkness shall fall away from you. This is the mightiest of all mighty powers for it conquers all that is fine and penetrates all that is coarse: thus was the world created. Thus in this very manner, wondrous aggregations come about. This is why I am called Hermes the Thrice Greatest, for I am possessed of three parts of wisdom of the universe. Accomplished is what I have announced to the sun's labor.

Heaven and earth are interrelated. Earth is created in the image of heaven. If we discover God's system in creating our world, we are free to reorganize that world! Separate earth from fire, and the fine from the coarse. If we distill the heart of the matter, the essence from the matter itself, and extract this *inner soul* of the metal, we can also make it grow and multiply. But we must do it "gently and with great sagacity."

The three aspects of universal wisdom are sun, moon, and man's ingenuity. Democrit, in *Physica et Mystica,* discloses that the key is "a stone which carries within itself the *seeds* of the two precious metals, capable of reproducing them, called the *philosopher's stone.*" As you refine base metal until it emerges pure gold, so you purify souls until they reach perfection. As the secrets of the retort are handed down from adept to adept, so the inner meanings of alchemy are passed on from priest to priest in a hermetic chain that permits no outsiders. The vessel being hermetically sealed may well be *us.* Gold is a living thing containing a *seed.* By using certain medicines, the seed can be made to grow. That medicine is the elixir or philosopher's stone.

The process is relatively simple: the stone is projected, that is, brought into contact with a base substance. Every metal is only a different version of the "prime matter," which contains a philosopher's stone. One need only find the prime matter, and extract the philosopher's stone from it.

Aristotle held that the universe consists of four basic elements: fire, water, air, and earth. Adepts called them the four essences, and added a fifth—*quinta essentia,* the quintessence, or elixir, the philosopher's stone.

Each of the four elements has two basic characteristics, moisture and heat. Fire is hot and dry, earth cold and dry, water cold and moist, and air hot and moist.

One of the two basic characteristics is more dominant than the other. In earth dryness represents the characteristic attribute; with water it is coldness; with air, moisture; and with fire, heat. In addition to the dominant character, each element contains a second aspect. When one of the secondary aspects is changed, then the element is *transmuted* into another element. Consider fire, whose dominant character is heat. It can lose its dryness in exchange for moisture and turn into steam. Air is predominantly moist. If it loses heat and takes on cold, water will result by condensation. Water, a cold element, loses its liquid state and turns into "earth," that is, solid ice. When earth, characterized by dryness, loses its secondary aspect of coldness, it becomes fire. Dry spells cause fires and solid bodies turn into smoke through the presence of fire.

This system also works in reverse. When earth loses its dry condition, it becomes water. When coldness is extracted from water, the result is air, the liquid evaporates. When air loses its moisture, fire can result. Only the form changes. Matter remains *immutable*.

The adepts felt, however, that prime matter could be changed from one state to another by two major principles, sulfur and mercury, and that *all* metals were composed of those two. Sulfur relates to fire, gold, and the sun; mercury to water, silver, and the moon. The sun is male, the moon female. In the secret philosophy of the adepts, sulfur corresponds to the mind, mercury to the soul; but a third element—body—was to be found in salt, also relating to earth. Symbols must be used in describing the *great task,* lest outsiders learn the inner secrets. A dragon signifies quicksilver. But the spiritual essence of quicksilver is needed to proceed with the "great work," the metal must *lose* its nature with the help of the *green dragon, aqua regis,* a powerful liquid, the *royal water,* which dissolves even gold!

In the *hermetic egg,* the retort, the "great work" takes place. Many steps lead to it. First, *incineration* of the metal mercury in the presence of oxygen, to obtain a powder from that metal. The second step is called the *decay.* Lead is purified through the destruction of its normal state. What remains behind in the vessel is like the soul at death of the body. Third, evaporation or refinement, in which a solid is extracted from a retort through the process of evaporation. However, the apparatus must be arranged in such a way that the substance solidifies again on the other end. Fourth, the *solution,* consists of the amalgamation of silver or gold in the presence of mercury, through smelting. Fifth, the *distillation,* in which a liquid is turned into steam in the retort, then condensed by cooling. By a continuous process of evaporation and condensation of the substance in a *sealed vessel,* the substance is purified.

In the sixth step, *solidification,* or *fixation,* a liquid is turned into a solid: sulfur is brought together with liquid mercury and turned into cinnabar. Fusion of the spiritually accented sulfur with spiritually activated mercury is like a mystical wedding, symbolic of the fusion of male and female, without which the great work cannot be accomplished. The seventh step, *extraction,* concerns the astrological conditions of the experiment.

But the seven basic chemical steps are only part of the process by which the great work is attained. There are five more stages. *Digestion* means a solid body is being dissolved in liquid. *Separation* softens a solid body to a pliable state, and in the tenth stage, *fermentation,* the substance is prepared for the final two processes, *multiplication* and *projection.* Multiplication is transmutation of a base metal into a precious metal, while increasing its quantity. Application of the tincture or elixir to base metal results not in an identical amount of precious metal, but in more. Finally, projection is the ultimate step by which the base metal is turned into solid gold, or, in spiritual terms, the soul becomes one with the divine principle.

Once the great work is accomplished, the philosopher's stone vanishes. It is no longer required. When man attains ultimate knowledge, he leaves earth behind. Gold returns to the earth, recommencing the cycle in the material dimension. Man's "immortal essence" returns whence it came, to be reborn again, recast in another form: an eternal life cycle in which there is neither beginning nor end.

I had heard references to Hermetic Lodges existing in America, but not until I read Hans Holzer's *The New Pagans* did I realize there was a group flourishing in Pasadena, California, called O.T.A.—Order Temple of Ashtart. Lest this conjure up visions of lascivious services in honor of the love goddess, let me assure you that the O.T.A. is a hermetic order that practices "magick" in the Western mystical tradition. "Hermetic" is a term derived from Hermes and goes back to the first and second century of our era, when a new philosophy based largely on Greek and late Egyptian ideas came into fashion. Basically, it teaches that "the human soul can only escape from its bondage to matter if it possesses the true knowledge or understanding [gnosis], which is the privilege of a select few," according to Olof Gigon in *Man, Myth, and Magic*.

The hermetic reaches out to God through mystical experience. If by certain rituals man extends himself beyond bodily limits and the limitations of space and time, he will know God. This, then, is essentially an intellectual approach to liberation and oneness with the deity by use of the path of mysticism.

O.T.A. practices the entire spectrum of what they refer to as "high magick," but they do not engage in the practice of black magic or anything that might have harmful results. Much of their ritual is Kabalistic and represents amalgamation of the ancient Hebrew mystic traditions, evocation of demons in the medieval manner, with hermetic ideals.

The O.T.A. is a hermetic-Rosicrucian Lodge in the Western occult tradition. Their theurgy derives from the "Clavicles of Solomon" and the Kabalistic system of the Order of the Golden Dawn; they claim to be heirs to the Gnostic tradition of the Ordo Templi Orientis through the dispensation of their late senior advisor, the Hon. Louis T. Culling. However, they should not be confused with the orthodox O.T.O., which still exists as a separate order, having several enclaves claiming valid warrants. Although they are masters of the O.T.O.'s "Great Rite," they do not emphasize it as the central theme of their "Magick." Their operations are primarily derived from the *Lemegaton*, a medieval grimoire that calls for rituals in "The Grand Manner," with all the drama and panoply of traditional wizardry. They employ their own secret Phoenician Kabala in preference to the Enochian system for advanced work in the Ordo Rosae Crucis.

The order is sponsored by the Church of the Hermetic Sciences, a California religious corporation chartered on October 23, 1970. The church is nondenominational and does not proselytize a dogma or revelation. The O.T.A. is secret and initiatory, but not clandestine. Candidates must present themselves to the Chapter House where they wish to affiliate and gain the unanimous approval of the membership, whose officers then submit their petitions to the Grand Lodge for final approval. Applicants must be between eighteen and fifty years of age, in good health, with no physical handicaps, felony record, or history of mental illnesses.

The order concentrates on the ancient rites of magick in their original form. From the Great Circle, the Magus conjures to visible appearance such entities as the goddess Astarte, the god Baal, and other mythological personifications in the Triangle of Art by ritual-hypnotic techniques that are authentic and effective. Such operations are performed in accordance with the principles of the Holy Kabala, and the precepts of this arcane philosophy must be understood. Advanced operations involve assumption of these god-forms, the Great Rite of Divine Congrex, and attainment of the Knowledge and Conversation of the Holy Guardian Angel. Astral journeys to the inner spheres of the Yetzirah Dimension are conducted by adepts, previous incarnations are investigated by deductive and inductive methods; they experiment with astral time travel—but they do not insist that their members "believe" in any dogmatic interpretation of such experiences. Their attitude is more philosophical than religious.

Ceremonial magick is not a science but rather an art. It combines the talents of the poet, the dramatist, and the artist with the wisdom of the great philosophers, resulting in a unique practical development of man's most potent intangible resource: his creative imagination.

Professor Hans Holzer vividly describes his initiation into the Order:

Presently, the master returned resplendent in a different kind of robe. Just like the others, he wore a hood over his head, but there was a large rose cross on his chest, and in his hand he carried a two-pointed spear, his mace of office as master. The time was at hand, and one by one we followed him into the other room. After we had all taken our positions inside and outside the great circle, the gong was struck by Frater Khedemel and the ritual began. For about two minutes the congregation intoned the vowels i, e, a, o, u in deep sonorous voices, while walking around the magic circle. The letters stand for the name of God. I took my place just inside the circle with my back toward the master, looking straight toward the great mirror, which was now uncovered. The glass became visible in the dim candlelight. The master then thrust two long candlesticks into my hand and motioned me to hold them up so that I could see the mirror more clearly. After some conjuration in kabbalistic Hebrew, the four archangels were invoked to stand guard in front of the circle, in back of the circle, to the right and left of the circle. This corresponds to the invocation of the four quarters or the Ancient Ones of Wicca. Now the master started to summon Baal to "come from whatever part of the world you are in and answer our questions. Manifest that which we desire . . . presently . . . we summon thee in the name of . . . and thy mother Ashtarot . . . we summon thee by thy middle name Tetragramaton. . . ." For about fifteen minutes the master repeated the invocation summoning the apparently unwilling spirit of Baal to manifest. At first gently, later somewhat more threateningly, he commanded Baal to appear. The tone of his voice, the atmosphere of the temple, and me standing there with two lighted candles and arms outstretched in front of the mirror were pure magic in its theatrical application. As I stood there staring into the half-darkened mirror, I thought I *felt* some sort of presence hovering over my shoulder. I did not see the clearly defined face of King Baal next to me in the glass, but I felt *something*.

11
Curses, Fact or Fantasy?

The fifth century B.C. tragic poet Aeschylus used a popular story of the curse laid upon the family of an ancient king named Atreus as the basis for a cycle of three plays called the *Oresteia*. Unfortunately, we don't know how much of the story of the "Curse of the House of Atreus" is historically factual. Strangely enough, the power of curses is the same as that of blessings. The ancient terms of malediction and benediction bear witness to the close similarity of the effort involved. Of course, it is true that the negative is more powerful than the positive since it involves, at times, great amounts of hatred within the individual performing the magic act called cursing. To summon similarly strong emotional impacts when blessing an individual is rarely possible.

Karl Spiesberger, a leading occult researcher, points out that curses are very real things. Curses represent thoughts. Thoughts cannot only create action by their very existence, but are, in fact, also generating thought forms, which he calls psychogones.

The basic theory behind the effectiveness of curses is fairly simple. When a person formulates a certain phrase containing strong emotional expressions of hatred, that person is, in actuality, creating thought forms that are both tangible and indestructible. The thought form imbued with the destructive purpose is then sent out either generally or specifically toward one or more individuals. It is not necessary for the receiver of the curse to be aware of it. Since the thought form is in itself a *tangible thing,* it is effective regardless of the receiver's attitude or position. In a sense, then, curses operate somewhat along the lines as dangerous radiation. When a radioactive agent sends

forth radioactive emanations, those radioactive particles reach individual human beings and cause certain
reactions, frequently damaging. Radiation coats objects
as well as people and frequently remains in the atmosphere for long periods of time. By the same token,
curses simply do not die away but fade very gradually,
both electronically when the energy created is dissipated
over great stretches of time, and emotionally when the
original purpose of the curse has been fulfilled. In this
respect, then, curses differ greatly from radiation. This
is connected with the basic motivation of the curse,
which is effective only if the person uttering the curse
is truly motivated by strong emotional feelings, generally great hatred, despair, or anger. Curses uttered in
jest or without true conviction are completely ineffective. That is why empty phrases containing words like
"I'll be damned" or "Damn you" are of no significance
and do not contain any danger.

Note that when certain religions proscribe the use of
the name of the deity in vain, they do so not because
there might be actual damage to the one using God's
name without good reason, but purely on dogmatic
grounds. Invoking the deity without cause is in viola-
tion of proper religious procedure.

Words by themselves are the framework of thought
forms. They can differ greatly in their effectiveness according to the mood in which they are uttered. A
highly tensed-up individual filled with hatred or anger
is a most powerful source of electromagnetic energy.
That temporarily very strong energy reserve is condensed by the cursing person into a comparatively
small number of words, which in turn create the
thought forms sent toward the one for whom the curse
is destined. Thus, by compressing a very large psychic
force into a very small "container," that container—
the curse—becomes very powerful indeed. Spiesberger
and other psychic researchers have shown, by citing
valid examples, that curses are far from figments of the
imagination. They are, in fact, very real energy sources
that must be reckoned with. Curses not only direct
themselves toward human beings, they can touch animals or even inanimate objects. They can be directed

toward entire towns or lands. Curses have been found to be effective against generations of people including many innocent descendants of the original wrongdoers.

There are two basic groups of curses. The one uttering the malediction can formulate his curse in general terms or it can be exactly tailored to one individual whom the cursor wishes to reach. In the case of the former, general group of curses, anyone coming into contact with the accursed person, persons, places, or objects will be affected by it. In some cases, general curses are merely protection against unauthorized interference such as with the Egyptian royal tombs.

But there is a third group of curses that is even more powerful than the other two. That is when the one originating the curse is not satisfied with drawing the utmost of his own energies of hatred and anger from the depth of his self and formulating them into words but invokes the powers of darkness as well to support him in his negative quest. This is done by following certain ritual magical formulas and can be understood or undertaken only by those well versed in the black arts. By combining his own forces with outside energies derived from the psychic world around him, the magician then forges a thunderbolt of hatred that is both extremely effective and difficult to discover. It is even more difficult to counteract.

But a curse has its boundaries. To begin with, any curse reaching its objective and having done what it was meant to do will of itself collapse into nothingness. For example, if a curse has been uttered to strike down a certain family's male members, then upon the death of the last heir the curse will disappear.

Beyond this, there is the law of karma, which is superior to any curse. If a curse would interfere with the proper karma of an individual, then the curse would be altered or made ineffective. Simply put, if no misdeed has been accomplished and yet a curse is uttered against an innocent individual, then that curse will not work. The karmic law requires that every deed be compensated for by another deed. No one need be afraid of being cursed if his conscience is clear. Conversely, if an evil deed has been perpetrated and the perpetrator has been cursed, he has every reason to expect the curse to be effective. That, too, is part of the basic karmic law of retribution.

In case where the receiver of the curse is made aware of it and wishes to blunt its effectiveness, he has another avenue open. By expressing pure love toward the one who has cursed him, a man can at least influence the effectiveness of the curse. The more love is poured out toward the perpetrator of the curse, the more likely it is to become ineffective. By the same token, if knowledge of an existing curse leads to great anxiety or even an attempt to run away from the curse, this will only result in greater effectiveness of the curse.

On the surface at least, the result of successful curses seems to be within the natural law and could perhaps be explained by a chain of misfortunes not necessarily connected with one another. Taken in the context of a known curse, however, they become part and parcel of a deliberate attempt to take revenge on those who have perpetrated a crime in the past, and frequently on their descendants. Curses can occur among the rich and the poor, the powerful and the humble. Just as the motivation for uttering a curse can differ widely among individuals, so the incidence of curses is spread among every culture, every type of social background. It is just that curses paid on prominent families or individuals, I learned, are more likely to come to public attention than something Aunt Minnie said against her landlady for cheating her!

Professor Hans Holzer, in *The Habsburg Curse,* traces the curse leveled against one of Europe's most distinguished royal dynasties back to its origin in the eleventh century. He examines the many branches of the Habsburg dynasty; explores, with the aid of well-known sensitivities, the castles and battlegrounds where ill-fated dramas were enacted; and pursues the malediction down through successive generations to its apparent demise in the twentieth century. Murder, suicide, mysterious disappearances, and madness—all were manifestations of what Professor Holzer demonstrates to be the result of a magnetic, evil force: the original Habsburg Curse.

He reports how the English magazine *Prediction* led him to the ancient Habsburg Curse, and he discovered that it all started way back in the twelfth century, when one of the early Habsburgs violated a country girl—the distraught girl may have uttered a curse against Count Habsburg and his family, taking the hawks in the yard as her witnesses. As long as there is a Habsburg left alive, there will be birds around the castle, but when the curse has finally found its mark, the birds will leave as a sign that it is all over. (The idea that birds cannot exist in an atmosphere of death is not new. Dark-colored or blackbirds are considered bearers of ill fortune or destiny in many civilizations. During eclipses, birds sometimes cannot sing or move about freely. In an atmosphere heavily laden with guilt and fear, highly sensitive birds may indeed find themselves disturbed and leave. It has been shown that birds have strong psychic sensitivity, and there may be some truth to this occult imagery.) Nine hundred years after the original curse was uttered, the Habsburgs are reduced to being just another old family. For the past few years their lives have been uneventful and fulfilled. Could it be that the curse found its mark with the death of Emperor Charles I and the loss of the thrones of Austria and Hungary?

To this day, juju works very smoothly in the deepest jungles of Africa. The record shows that many people have died as a result of direct intervention by a magician, without ever realizing that this was taking place.

Much more so than in the Western world, African curses depend on elements of fear and ostracism for added effectiveness. Nearly always, the victim is informed that a curse has been uttered, usually in a roundabout way to increase the uncertainty of the matter and to prevent the victim from arguing the originator of the curse out of his anger. But associating with an accursed person is equally undesirable, consequently it is customary to let the community know as well that so-and-so has been cursed. The victim will find himself isolated, and sometimes the curse takes effect in a manner not relying on magic but on brutal force, when someone in the community does away with the accursed person to protect the other from the effect of the curse.

The curse of the House of Cowdrey is well known in English folklore. It is an example of the difficulty inherent in timing—and thus being in some way prepared for—the culmination of a curse. Cowdrey was once owned by a family named Browne, of which line one Sir Anthony Browne succeeded to the property in 1543 at the death of his half-brother. Sir Anthony was a favorite among Henry VIII's retainers and was elevated to the honorable positions of Master of the Horse and Chief Standard Bearer. At that time, Henry, branded by Rome a damned renegade, busied himself dissolving the papal spheres of influence in England by confiscating and giving as gifts to his loyal followers the vast and opulent estates of the monasteries. To Anthony was given the estate and all the the buildings of Battle Abbey. When the reconstruction was completed, Anthony hosted a great festivity that had the whole countryside coming in to "warm the house." Amid the revelry, an uninvited monk muscled his way to the lord's table and, grim with fury, cursed the man and his entire lineage for his desecration of the holy temple. The monk pronounced the following as punishment for Anthony's transgressions: that by fire and water would the house of Cowdrey and the line of Anthony Browne be destroyed. "By water," through drowning, died the foremost male of the lineage—but what of the fire? The words of the centuries-old curse were later recalled: Cowdrey Castle burned to the ground because a scullery maid was clumsy with her bucket of coals.

Astrologer-historian Arthur Gatti, in *The Kennedy Curse,* analyzes thirty individual Kennedy charts and concludes that no evil witch crashed any of the christenings, but a kind of curse does haunt the Kennedy family fortunes, bringing with it extraordinarily bad luck. Besides indications of great personal gifts, ambition, wealth, and power, the charts are full of signs of confusion, hard choices, self-sacrifice, illness, disaster, grief, guilt, enemies, and *hidden conspiracies!*

12

Magic, Witchcraft, and Sex

It is of course wrong to call anyone who can predict things, or who knows things he couldn't possibly know, or who performs feats now classed as extrasensory perception, a "witch," as people still do occasionally. They may do so in ignorance or in jest but it should be remembered that no one is a witch who is not either a member of a practicing witch coven, or, if working alone, has studied and practiced the tenets of the Old Religion thoroughly and for some time.

Much has been written, and even more rumored, about the connection between sex and witchcraft, very little of it corresponding to fact. There is, first of all, the notion that witchcraft rites are predominantly sexy, and it is this idea that both attracts some people and repels others. Those who are attracted to witchcraft rites because they expect an orgy had better stay away to begin with, for if it is anything at all, witchcraft is a spiritual-intellectual "thing," not a flesh concourse.

Anyone even slightly familiar with the teachings of the Old Religion will recognize its insistence on "perfect couples" in the rites and its reluctance to admit single people on their own. This is not out of false prudery but because the witches know how much better people work when they work in unison and with both spiritual and physical closeness. Witches are concerned with results, not with morals. Promiscuity and *over-emphasis* of the sexual aspects would hinder rather than help the results of the circle, so naturally they do not care for it. The tensions engendered by one person about the sexual aspect of another to whom he or she is not yet close are bound to detract from the overall effort put forth by the group, and consequently are usually discouraged.

Public opinion sometimes confuses aspects of Satanism with witchcraft. But witches do believe in marital fidelity and do not worship erotic symbols on their lowest, physical level at all. The very ancient fertility aspects of the cult are purely religious in that the man's reproductive organs are worshiped as symbols of creativity. Every human culture has at one time or another worshiped such symbols and felt such thoughts important in their relationship with the deity. To consider fertility cults dirty or daring is to have a distorted point of view—either one's own false values, or biased attitudes instilled in one by a church or religion hostile to natural sexual expression and procreation. This latter thought is not so farfetched when one considers the repressive attitudes of medieval Christianity, and, to a degree, also of Islam, toward anything dealing openly with the expression of sex, and toward praise of the woman as an equal partner in a man's world. Women, the principal vessels of the sex drive, were relegated to an inferior and hidden position where their role could be controlled rigidly and confined to the absolute minimum to keep the human race going.

But witchcraft treats women as equals of men, in some cults even as superiors, and that in itself is a unique position among the world's religions and perhaps is also responsible for the strong appeal the Craft has nowadays to women.

Apart from the supposed sexy aspects of the rites themselves, the Old Religion is also reputed to have powers to increase sexual potency, make charms and love spells, and contribute in unorthodox ways to the sexual desires of its practitioners. There is nothing supernatural about this, either. Through advanced knowledge of nature's herbs and plants, certain drugs have long been known to be useful as aphrodisiacs, and witches simply learned to use them.

Recently I saw an ad reading, "See Pagan Rites in Full Technicolor" on a New York City movie marquee. What the victim of subliminal and not-so-subliminal advertising saw inside the motion-picture house was nothing more than a lesson in anthropology: documentary films taken among the primitive tribes of New Guinea or Africa were being touted as something forbidden, exciting, and bound to get you all shook up! The fact of the matter was that these rites were far from unusual *for the people performing them,* who do not view life by Western standards. But far more importantly, the primitive people of New Guinea and Africa are not pagans in the true sense of the word. The misuse of this term is somewhat similar to the abuse of the word *native.* Everyone born someplace is a native of that country. Yet, when we speak of "natives" we often think of such people as being primitive or in need of colonial enlightenment. By the same token "pagan" means nothing more than "coming from the country." *Pagus* in Latin is a term applied to the provinces in general, as different from the cities.

The impression that witchcraft has sex as its preeminent feature persists. In 1969 the *News of the World,* a London newspaper, published a series of articles that lumped together witchcraft, ritual magic, the Black Mass, and the desecration of church yards by vandals. During the course of this series the paper uncovered the fact that a schoolteacher-priest had planned to hold Black Masses using virgins as an altar, that a couple in the Isle of Man exposed their young daughter to the danger of moral corruption by allowing her to attend naked coven meetings, and that a West London housewife had been the prime mover at similar coven meetings for years without the knowledge of her husband. If the first two allegations were true, of course, the *News of the World* performed a public service by exposing them. But by and large the articles tended to overdo the sexual aspects.

If the evidence at the witch trials of the Middle Ages is to be believed, it is then undeniably true that sex played a major part in the witchcraft of other times; it is also true that sex plays no small part in the activities of certain occult groups today. But there are factors which inhibit the modern witch in the pursuit of unlicensed sexual excess. A great deal of whirling and dancing goes on at the average coven meeting, leading to a state of almost total exhaustion. Frank Smyth, an English writer, quotes a coven member thusly: "The object of dancing around, originally, was to work up excitement and sexual energy which, uninhibited by clothing, projected an almost tangible emotional sensation which the witches call the 'cone of power.' In fact I have scarcely ever seen a male witch with an erection after such a communal dance."

Anyway, witches rarely thrust their sexual attentions on any outsider, just as they refrain from pushing their religious views. But modern witchcraft, like any other emotive concern, has been exploited by the unscrupulous. So-called black magic groups that persuade newcomers to undress and indulge in all kinds of grotesque sexual activity, secretly photograph them, and then use the photographs for blackmail, are not unknown in most large cities. Also, overt or covert prostitution is sometimes the purpose of magic-cum-witchcraft circles. Because the great advantage of ritual is that it can take many forms, any perverted but imaginative mind could invent ceremonies cloaked in a quasi-mystical veil of mumbo-jumbo that would make most witch cults look rather tame.

If anything, I've found the erotic element, while certainly always present, couched in poetic language. According to the father of modern witchcraft, Dr. Gerald Gardner, the fertility rituals are symbolic as well as actual. Here is his "magical legend of the witches."

Now G. [the Witch Goddess] had never loved, but she would solve all the Mysteries, even the Mystery of Death; and so she journeyed to the Nether Lands.

The Guardians of the Portals challenged her: "Strip off thy garments, lay aside thy jewels; for nought may ye bring with ye into this our land."

So she laid down her garments and her jewels, and was bound, as are all who enter the Realms of Death by the Mighty One. (Note: There was a Celtic custom of binding corpses. The cord which had bound a corpse was useful in learning the "second sight.")

Such was her beauty that Death himself knelt and kissed her feet, saying, "Blessed be thy feet that have brought thee in these ways. Abide with me, let me but place my cold hand on thy heart."

She replied, "I love thee not. Why dost thou cause all things that I love and take delight in to fade and die?"

"Lady," replied Death, " 'tis Age and Fate, against which I am helpless. Age causes all things to wither; but when men die at the end of time, I give them rest and peace, and strength so that they may return. But thou, thou are lovely. Return not; abide with me."

But she answered, "I love thee not."

Then said Death, "An' thou received not my hand on thy heart, thou must receive Death's scourge."

"It is Fate; better so," she said, and she knelt, and Death scourged her, and she cried, "I feel the pangs of love."

And Death said, "Blessed be," and gave her the Fivefold Kiss, saying, "thus only may ye attain to joy and knowledge."

And he taught her all the Mysteries. And they loved and were one, and he taught her all the Magics.

For there are three great events in the life of man; Love, Death, and Resurrection in a new body; and Magic controls them all. For to fulfill love you must return again at the same time and place as the loved one, and you must remember and love them again. But to be reborn you must die, and be ready for a new body; and to die you must be born; and without love you may not be born. And these be all the Magics.

St. Louis, Missouri, once called the Gateway to the West, has a fair share of occult activities. At one time there was a Gardnerian coven, which may or may not still flourish. Its activities, however, are now overshadowed by the School of Wicca at nearby St. Charles, Missouri. This is due to the fact that its founders and directors, Gavin and Yvonne Frost, have recently been very much involved in the news, at least in the occult news, because of controversy arriving from their first book, *The Witch's Bible*.

Yvonne was born a Baptist. She was working as a secretary in the aerospace business in southern California five years ago. While attending spiritual development classes with a local spiritualist church, she became exposed to the idea of communication with the beyond. Seances and meditation followed, and after she met her present husband, Gavin, who had always been interested in witchcraft, she became involved in the ancient belief.

Professor Hans Holzer questioned the Frosts about the sexual aspects of their initiation rites.

"Do you use sexual energy to raise the cone of power?"

"We think that the cone of power is raised through the excitement of the dance and through its sexual feelings, not through orgasm."

"I believe you have been criticized for the use of artificial phalli?"

"But phalli have been used in the Craft for many years. We feel that a young girl about to be married should be prepared for it. We use wooden phalli, a small one and a larger one, and it is a muscle-training device. If the girl is initiated into the Craft, then the phallus is returned to the fire, but if she is married in a normal wedding ceremony then it is just thrown away."

"Why is an artificial phallus used when obviously it could be done in the natural way by a man?"

"This is the girl's first experience with sex, her muscles are tight, and she has never been stretched in any way before. This is actually preceding any sex, and it would apply only in the case of a virgin."

To say that Gardner was a nudist and, therefore, that his version of witchcraft is performed in the nude, as some people both inside and outside of the Craft have said, is a moot point: my research indicates that witchcraft rituals, especially the high rituals, were *always* performed in the nude. While it is true that ordinary social gatherings, or perhaps Esbats, were attended by witches wearing their best finery, it is also true that high-holiday celebrations—that is, the four major Sabbaths and the final stages of minor rituals— were always performed "skyclad." Those who would deny this are merely covering up their own sexual hangups. If anything, Dr. Gardner's interest in nudity stemmed from witchcraft, not the other way around. The reason why witches go nude can be found in the belief that body electricity cannot escape for the necessary ritual if contained by wool, such as in clothing, but also, from a philosophical point of view, the lack of clothing makes everyone equal before the Mother Goddess. As for erotic elements in rituals, we must again keep in mind that much is in the eye of the beholder. In societies such as ours, sexual practices for religious purposes are still frowned upon, even among many witches who are unable to shake themselves loose from their upbringing in another religion or their environmental pressures.

The greatest psychic power imaginable is raised in sexual intercourse between two fully attuned partners. This, of course, is the crux: the partners must be truly in tune, one with the other; they must be psychically, physically, and spiritually aware of their purpose and never lose sight of the reasons for their sexual union. If sex is the excuse for practicing witchcraft, it is perversion; but if sex is used for ritual purposes by properly prepared people, it can contribute to the overall results of the ritual far beyond anything that purely intellectual efforts or ritualistic movements may furnish. We must remember that erotic elements were not objectionable to the ancients, who saw in the performance of sexual intercourse during a religious ritual a symbolic act encouraging the forces of nature to commit union likewise and thus make things grow. Every primitive religion contains such elements whether expressed symbolically or in actuality. Only by the fusion of the male and female element in nature, and thus also in man, does nature move forward. Ultimately, the polarity of things is the essential element. Through the interaction of male and female polarity, power results; or, if you prefer, by the union of the male and female polarities in a single effort, the original purpose of the power structure is fulfilled: for at the beginning there was neither male nor female, but one single force. Having been split into the female and male half, the two polarities have been trying to *rejoin* each other ever since.

I discovered that the so-called Fivefold Kiss ritual

is pretty stimulating to begin with. It goes like this (with appropriate action):

Blessed be thy feet that have brought thee in these ways.
Blessed be thy knees that shall kneel at the sacred altar.
Blessed by thy womb [phallus] without which we would not be.
Blessed by thy breast formed in beauty and strength.
Blessed be thy lips that shall speak the sacred names.

Hans Holzer quotes a "very ancient" Anglo-Saxon spell, which to me illustrates the feeling of erotic-ecstatic union with the Goddess rather well:

In love I come to Thee, O Mother Goddess, to fill me with the joys of life. Let there be union between thine own self and me and between my companion and me and let the union be so complete as to enshrine our trinity within and without; let the force of thy love permeate our bodies and minds, let the power raised from that union rise up to Thee so that thy works may be accomplished. I join hands with my companion in sacred union of body, mind and spirit, through which the power be raised; may the power thus raised be directed to———[predetermined purpose of ritual] and in token thereof, O Mother Goddess, instill into us your greatness, your splendor and your eternal wisdom, for the force of love is a force of life. As we come together and are one, the force within us is joined into a still greater force by the touch of your hands, O Mother Goddess, Protector of love. So mote it be.

13

Satanism
and Devil Worship

According to Rollo Ahmed (*The Black Art*), black magic goes back to antediluvian times. The occultist traces black magic back to the lost continent of Atlantis, which sank beneath the waves of the Western Ocean and thereby caused the greatest cataclysm the world has ever experienced, referred to in the Bible as the Flood. The people of Atlantis had reached a high state of evolution, physically, mentally, and spiritually, and had attained a vast knowledge of psychic powers. Unfortunately, they proceeded to misuse their powers, and the initiates of Atlantis fought one against the other for supernatural supremacy, using their powers for the enslavement of their fellow creatures and the race as a whole. They supposedly reached an even higher standard of civilization than man has since attained. But they also became adepts of the black art and controlled psychic and elemental forces to dominate the animal and mineral kingdoms. This race is symbolized in the Bible as the Tower of Babel, a civilization whose base rested on earth and whose summit reached into higher realms than man was yet entitled to penetrate. In the end, the Atlanteans brought about their own destruction by the perversion of forces that destroyed the entire continent.

Nowadays, it is no longer illegal to worship the devil. Probably the best known Satanic leader in America is Anton Sandor La Vey. Hans Holzer, in *The Truth About Witchcraft,* describes vividly how he met the quixotic Satanist at his San Francisco temple:

> The house is painted black from the top of the roof to the last window shutter. Even from the outside it

looks peculiar: one of those turn-of-the-century private residences San Francisco is full of. This one stands on California street, 'way out toward the ocean, about a half-hour by taxi from the downtown area with its sophisticated hotels and shops. Anton La Vey is a realist, on the other hand. Originally a wild-animal trainer with a circus, he later became a police photographer and is a good enough organist to play professionally. It all came in handy in the Satanist movement; the organ playing could set the right sinister mood, and his old connection with the police department was helpful to stay unmolested while at the same time assuring him protection from idle curiosity seekers. Paintings of traditional representations of hell, haunted houses, and devils adorned the walls, They were remarkably fine paintings, and the works of the high priest himself. The table was a marble slab which used to be a tombstone and still bore the inscription of the late gentleman whose earthly remains it once guarded. A skeleton leered at us from a glass cabinet in the corner and stuffed owls completed the atmospheric feeling. Soon the high priest himself arrived, wearing black pants and a black leather jacket. His face was deliberately made to appear devilish by the removal or cropping of all hair on top and the addition of a small beard. La Vey did indeed look the part.

Later that day, the amiable artist-high-priest was a totally different person. The house also seemed different . . . the decorations no longer looked like whimsical touches of a tongue-in-cheek devil worshipper, but as authentic relics closely tied to the ritual about to be performed.

By midnight, the room was filled with fifteen or sixteen congregation members. They were young and old and looked like a good cross-section of San Franciscans. Mainly men had come that night, and a goodly number of them wore small beards, perhaps in honor of their high priest. The small number of women present were average type. They all sat on folding chairs toward the rear of the room. In front of them was an altar occupied by the stretched-out body of a young woman covered by a leopardskin. A man completely covered with a black hooded robe with slits for the eyes entered the room. He was followed by four or five other men similarly dressed, who stayed a little behind. With one quick gesture, the man in the black hood yanked the leopardskin off the girl on the altar. She was, of course, nude. Her head rested comfortably on a specially built neck rest while her feet dangled somewhat over the other end of the altar. The light, provided by candles only, was sufficiently bright to highlight her body even to those seated in the rear of the room.

Now one of the other black-robed fellows handed the leader a small cup. Someone played the organ all during this opening ceremony, but it was not, of course, La Vey himself, who had not yet appeared among his flock. The music was properly atmospheric and reminded one of the old background music for Hiss the Villain in an old-time music hall. The cup, it developed, contained a mixture of semen and urine, the Satanists' answer to holy water. With a dispenser in the shape of a human phallus, the man in the black hood then sprinkled the congregation with this mixture, while a bell rang in short intervals to announce the opening of the service. The stage was set for the entrance of the high priest, Anton Sandor La Vey.

After the appropriate organ music cue, he strode in with showmanly stance, dressed in a tight-fitting black headpiece with red horns and wearing a black robe over black leotards. Taking the sword from the high priestess, he addressed the four corners of the room. "In nomine dei Satanas, Lucifer excelsi! In the name of our great god, Satan Lucifer, the ruler of the Stygian pits, I command thee to come forth out of the black realms. Come forth, in the name of the four dark princes of hell, Satan! Lucifer! Belial! Leviathan! Satan, take the chalice of ecstasy . . . which is filled with the elixir of life . . . and instill it with the power of the Black Magic . . . which diffuses and supports the universe. . . ." With that, the high priest was handed a chalice from which he drank a toast to the Prince of Darkness. He then placed the chalice right on top of the pubic area of the girl on the altar, where it rested comfortably for the rest of the service.

But I discovered that Satanists—in La Vey's terms —are not true materialists either, for they do believe in a life hereafter. To them, surviving spirits are the forces of men unable to find enjoyment of their earthly lives and who must seek it beyond the body. The life force continues in existence beyond death, and to the Satanists this proves that using it fully while still in the flesh is the proper thing to do. La Vey took pains to point out that the First Satanist Church of San Francisco should not be confused with medieval superstitions or worse. No unbaptized babies are killed in the rites, no ritual murder takes place, and no Black Mass. This is a cult dedicated to the enjoyment of worldly pleasures free from all restrictions, guilt feelings, or, hell forbid, original sin. Satanists do not believe in a personal devil as a living individual. Their devil is the *devil within* every man, that part of his nature that longs for full enjoyment of worldly pleasures. By invoking Satan, his congregation was merely calling upon its own unconscious desires to encourage their fulfillment.

I also discovered that the symbol of Satan is the *inverted* pentagram with the head of a goat in it. This represents the carnal nature of man as opposed to the spiritual element, which would be represented by the star right side up. Two horns pointed defiantly toward heaven, and three horns downward, representing the Trinity denied, are additional symbolisms of this emblem.

As for the sacrifice of *adult* human beings, they do not do this either, although La Vey admits they have many candidates for this practice. But they do it symbolically through "the hex."

Ever since Pope Paul declared publicly that the devil was a real person *to him,* and, of course, the antagonist of the Roman Catholic Church, clergymen all over the world and laymen with religious orientation have looked into the matter of the devil and whether or not he is in fact still among us. Gregory Peck, after doing the current movie *The Omen,* says he cannot believe the devil is a person. In fact, anyone seriously suggesting that there was such a thing as the devil as a person a scant ten years ago would have been looked at with horror, or a smile, depending upon the viewpoint of the onlooker. Today, austere publications have devoted many pages to this matter; the *New York Times* Magazine's article by Andrew M. Greeley, entitled "The Devil, You Say," rehashes much from the past, most of it false, some of it correct, to come to the conclusion that evil in man is really the kind of devil one should worry about. The author leaves unresolved the question of a personal devil, but points to the continued existence of evil in this world as certain proof that the forces of darkness do prevail at times.

According to Sigmund Freud, the devil is a father substitute for those who have no luck, are too poorly gifted, or are too ineffective to make a living. William Blatty's novel *The Exorcist,* allegedly based upon a real case in St. Louis in 1959, has given new impetus to the whole business of the reality of the devil. Catholic priests are divided between the acceptance of the reality of a personal devil and consider the business of demonic possession more properly treated by the psychiatrist. Pope Paul VI, in his recent address about evil and the devil, assured his listeners that he was convinced of "an intervention in us and in our world of an obscure agent, the devil. Evil is not merely a lack of something, but an effective agent, a living, spiritual being, perverted and perverting. A terrible reality. Mysterious and frightening." Is the devil a real person or a principle? In either case, the point is that the devil represents "the negative force."

Lamentably, the author of this article in the *New York Times* Magazine of February 4, 1973, Dr. Greeley, a Roman Catholic priest, is not as learned about the devil and his ways as one might have hoped from someone in his position. Quite correctly, he explains the origin of the word *Satan* as the Hebrew term for accuser or adversary. But Satanas is also the brother of God, the "demiurge" of Greek mythology, just as Seth is the brother of Osiris in the Egyptian pantheon. Dr. Greeley then assures us that the word *devil* comes from the Greek diabolos, while my learned witchcraft friends assure me that it comes from the gypsy term *divil,* meaning "stranger." He does not mention Samiel, another name given the devil by the ancient Hebrews. To Anton La Vey, Satan represents "vengeance— instead of turning the other cheek," and such human traits as indulgence, greed, selfishness, and the survival of the strong over the weak.

The people who call themselves Satanists today are "anti-witches"; that is, they use certain elements of witchcraft but pervert them to their own point of view, which is frequently diametrically opposed to that of witchcraft. Those who are truly devilworshipers in the worst sense of the term might lead a furtive existence in secret meeting places, indulging sick impulses that have very little to do with a true cult. They do not number many, either, but, unfortunately, their actions invite negative comment in the press. Whenever word is received that an animal has been sacrificed, or that murders have occurred, such as the Charles Manson affair, in which the perpetrators claimed Satanic impulses, the public is quick to lump all pagans into the same pot with those perverse individuals. There is a certain shock value in being able to say you're a devilworshiper or Satanist just as there is undoubtedly shock value in being a witch, but the impact of those words is based upon largely erroneous images. In the mind of the average person, witches and Satanists are evil, and practically the same. Only to those who understand the vast differences between a follower of the Old Religion and a Satanist, the images become separate and distinct.

I found a typical American example of a practicing warlock in Theodore J. Rabouin. In his late thirties, Mr. Rabouin lives in Westboro, Massachusetts, and has been a practitioner of his craft for about seven years. Mr. Rabouin explains that he was the seventh son of a seventh son, as was his grandfather before him, and attaches great significance to this fact. Furthermore, two of his great-great-great-grandfathers were executed for practicing witchcraft in Canada and France, so Mr. Rabouin considers himself a kind of hereditary warlock. Early in life he became obsessed with the study of the occult. He grew up in a house directly across the street from a cemetery in Worcester,

Massachusetts, and played among the graves the way other children play in streets. He is mainly self-educated because, as he puts it, he was too preoccupied with what is on the other side of the grave to worry about formal education. Today, Mr. Rabouin is an aide at a local hospital, working closely with psychiatrist M. Greenberg. He is not content with merely a "warlock," but has engaged in various psychic activities as well, such as an attempt to exorcise ghosts and using his ESP powers to "help" people. By his own admission, his involvement in the occult has rendered him more and more unworldly.

There lived, until his recent passing, a kindly old Satanist in Toledo, Ohio. His name was Dr. Herbert Sloane. He was a professional cardopractor (card reader) and former barber who gave tarot readings to those wishing to be told of their future. Herb Sloane had the personality and appearance of a vaudevillian of old. He was a kind and gentle person, full of humor and compassion for his fellow man. He had traveled the Middle West in detail and he had more friends in his home town of Toledo, Ohio, than some church men have in all of the United States.

Herb's strange religious convictions came to him in 1908. Although he was friendly to *all* witches, he worshiped the "Lord Sathanas." He was a witch of the Ophitic Gnostic Sect, and he practiced that strange religion for at least sixty-three years of his life. Witchcraft in Toledo was practiced mainly by two individuals, Herb Sloane and his Satanic group, and a charming lady by the name of Jeffery Cather. Ms. Cather runs a boutique of the unusual called Circe's Treasures. Here she sells anything from standard occult items to handsome candles, which are very beautiful and unusual, but she does not sell initiations or rituals, as far as I can determine; her witchcraft, it would appear, is her private affair. According to Herb Sloane, she is a fourth-generation hereditary witch and apparently Toledo was big enough for the two of them.

Hans Holzer describes the service Herb Sloane had invited him to, to celebrate the full moon of October. Proceedings were held in the Dragon Room, which also doubled as Herb's living quarters and covenstead. As for the Dragon Room, it looked best in semidarkness. With candles flickering, the "icons" (as Herb called the various pictures, photographs, and designs on the walls) looked rather impressive and gave the small, elongated room the feeling of a secret hiding place. Not the least of the items on the walls was a brass devil's mask mounted on a black plate.

Herb Sloane disappeared for a moment to get ready for the action. When he returned, he wore a black cape, and his impressive face was now crowned by two plastic horns, securely stuck onto his forehead. After a moment of hushed silence, Sloane took a deep breath and began the service by ringing a bell.

> Our Lady of Endor Coven of the Ophitic Gnostic Cult of Satanas is now in Sabbath, and this will be the order of service: the call, which you've just heard, the invocation, the creed, first reading, announcements, supplication, communion, second reading, sermon, benediction, and social hour. Let's bow our heads for the invocation. Lord Satanas, we invoke into this covenstead thy sacred presence this Sabbathnight, that thou be with us in understanding, that thou open our ears to hear and understand the things which we should understand, and close our ears and minds to those things which are not pleasing to thee. Thank you, Lord. Nema, Nema, Nema, Nema!

Of course, I realize that Nema is Amen spelled backwards.

When Anton La Vey became more and more successful, he founded subdivisions or "grottos" in various cities around the country. Eventually, as is the unfortunate habit of all religious groups, dissension arose in some of these groups and they split, one portion staying under the agis of High Priest Anton, the other going their own way. Thus it was in the case of the grotto at Dayton, Ohio. The group in Dayton is composed primarily of young people between the ages of eighteen and thirty. They are simple people; their everyday ways are no different from those of any Midwestern working person. John De Haven, a student and radio broadcaster, is their spiritual leader or "Magister Sacrorum." The group changed its name when it left the La Vey fold and became known as the Church of Satanic Brotherhood. The Dayton group publishes a newsletter in which articles pertaining to Satanic worship and excerpts from *The True Grimoire* are published, the latter being the medieval handbook of spell-casting and demonology.

John De Haven explained:

> The Church of the Satanic Brotherhood is a religious association of Satanists founded by members and former members of the Church of Satan who were attracted by the idea of a national fellowship of Satanists, but who felt that the Church of Satan did not serve this purpose. Our church is governed by a council, whose authority is balanced by the ceremonial head of our church, the high priest, the executive head of our church, the Magister Sacrorum, and the general council of all members.

What exactly is a Black Mass?

This is a blasphemous ceremony copying the Christian High Mass in every respect, except that everything is reversed. The crucifix is hung upside down, the altar is covered in black instead of white, candles are black, hymns are sung backward, the rite is performed by a defrocked priest, if possible, and whenever the name of the Lord or Christ is to be praised, it is spat upon in the Black Mass. Sexual rites in connection with the Black Mass are a more modern addition; originally this was strictly a religious "reversal" ceremony and nothing that did not occur in the real mass was parodied. There is a connection between Black Mass and devil worship in that the place of the Christ is taken by the Prince of Darkness. Black Masses were performed whenever special needs arose. Catherine de Medici ordered one celebrated when she tried to save the life of her husband, the King of France. He died despite the ritual killing of a child. The murder of children and the shedding of blood was a touch added to the mass in the late Middle Ages, but it was not a custom directly tied in with the mass itself.

144

Occasionally, animals were sacrificed. The sacrificial element perhaps derived from the alleged "doctrine" of devil worship—to do evil for its own sake and as a way to salvation.

Thus, devil worshipers actually were also victims of the Church's fantasies. Accepting the idea that there was indeed a devil, they merely switched sides. Instead of fearing him, they joined and worshiped him. Perversity was the key to their actions. All that Church and society considered good, they were to shun, while all evil deeds were stepping stones on their road to salvation in His image. Only when considered in this light do the acts of devil worshipers make some sense. They were and are not criminals as such, but misguided individuals following a belief that in itself is a program of destruction, and therefore a harmful force in our world.

To mock Christ was only a mild form of their faith; to commit all the sins the Christian Church stands against, and do this as often as possible, is a good deed in the eyes of the devil worshiper. Every form of sexual intercourse and perversion is encouraged, every physical excess, every form of materialistic greed. It is simply a reversal of accepted morality. Having already sunk as low as they possibly could in their lives, they had nothing to fear from hell after their deaths: they already were part of it.

These strange cultists were few and far between. Certainly, the accusations of witches being devil worshipers were totally false.

In the late eighteenth century, a group of English noblemen, bored with their lives of luxury and dissipation, looked for new and unusual thrills. They discovered, through old books, that devil worship might be the answer. The Hell Fire clubs of Georgian England were not really religion-oriented, but they did incorporate some of the blasphemous elements of true devil worship. Their sexual orgies, for instance, were always in the habits of monks and nuns, and their "sanctuary" near High Wycombe, not far from London, mimicked a church.

145

14
Exorcism

Perhaps no other phenomenon within psychic research has attracted so many divided opinions as possession. This is because it crosses over into the field of religion, and even into the area of psychiatry. Thus, it invites destructive criticism of those to whom these other fields are the only truths. Even today, very few psychiatrists are willing to accept nonphysical explanations for paranormal experiences. Even fewer religious individuals, firmly rooted in their particular beliefs, are willing to accept the psychic research view concerning possession. Thus, the researcher requires a certain neutral attitude when dealing with these complex phenomena. He must be committed neither to the orthodox scientific and psychiatric view that *all* paranormal experience is per se a symptom of emotional or mental illness—nor to those religions that hold that all experiences of possession are due to demonic influence and can only be explained by the involvement of the heaven-hell syndrome.

I wondered why there had been an increase in interest in phenomena of possession and obsession in recent years. It is hard to judge, because the occurrence of this type of case has been no more nor less than it had in previous years. Perhaps the increased attention given to phenomena of this kind stems from the general preoccupation of the public with occult phenomena and increasing awareness, especially by the young, of the powers of human personality not yet touched by conventional means. At a party last night a friend of mine pointed out that he feels all those people possessing extrasensory powers of any kind represent the beginning of a new awareness in people. Years ago the human eye could not see the entire spectrum of colors it sees today, thanks to instruments. Possession involves complex situations and cannot be dealt with lightly or by amateurs. Rightly, it deserves the attention it is getting nowadays, because it contains both dangerous and beneficial aspects.

The word *possession* comes from the Latin *possedere,* which means "to possess, to own, to take over." Taking the word's two components, however, we find possession consisting of *post* and *sedere.* The latter word means "to sit, to be situated," and the prefix "post" generally means "after" or "beyond." Thus, when we translate freely, *possedere,* means "to sit on top of." It is interesting to note in this connection that in the Middle Ages, a popular conception of possession included a wraith or gnome sitting on top of the possessed individual, pushing down upon the body, causing nightmares and other forms of altered states of consciousness. The concept of the word *possession* indicates that it relates to a total takeover, total control of an individual by another individual or some outside force. Possession excludes the will of the possessed. It presupposes the inability of the victim to overcome the attacking force and, in submitting to it, become its tool.

I continued my search in libraries to become more familiar with possession in terms of various approaches. I learned to distinguish between the medical, religious, popular, and, finally, parapsychological approach to the problem of possession. In a *medical* sense, the verdict is likely to be schizophrenia or some other form of mental derangement. The medical profession on the whole does not acknowledge the existence of separate entities apart from the flesh-and-blood personality of the victim. In fact, the medical experts barely recognize the possibility that man has something more than a physical body. Medicine has not yet come to terms with the problem of human personality-soul-spirit. In medical terms, then, the possibility of one person being possessed by another against his will is entirely inconceivable, with the sole marginal exception of hypnosis, of course, or some other form of undue but direct influence. When a person shows marked personality changes and acts in a way contrary to previous habits, the medical doctor will look for personality defects rather than the presence of a new or outside personality.

Possession in terms of the *religious establishment* is nothing but the entrance into the individual's soul of an outside force, generally evil. Whether or not the term demonic possession is used, the implication is that a living entity has entered the body of the victim in order to express his own will and frustrations. To the Church, this is always evil and must be dealt with through exorcists. Not every religious community accepts this version, but the orthodox faiths do believe in the existence of possession and the need for exorcism. To this day, the Roman Catholic Church retains the rite of exorcism. In an offshoot of Orthodox Judaism called the Hasidic cult, belief in the dybbuk, or possessing spirit, is still extant and is dealt with similarly as in the Roman Catholic exorcism. In both cases, the possessing spirit is asked to leave, and when it refuses, it is forced out of the body of the victim by various means. In earlier days these means included everything from torture to bizarre threats and incantations believed to be effective by the sheer power of the arrangement of phrases. When only words were used to drive out the evil spirits, it had either no effect at all, or, through a form of hypnotic suggestion, resulted in the freeing of the victim from his possessor. However, when physical torture was used and applied (in theory to the possessing entity, but in practice hurting the victim), the results were not as fortunate. The Church believed that the death of a possessed individual in the process of trying to free that person from his possessor was unavoidable if the evil spirit was stronger than the victim. The Church felt that it was better to destroy both than permit the victim to exist under the spell of his possessor and possibly harm others. The number of unfortunate people who were thus tortured to death by seemingly well-meaning exorcists of religious background is considerable. However, if the victim survived religious exorcism with his possessor intact, then clearly the exorcist had but two choices: destroy the victim altogether and thus take care of both the victim and possessor, or place the victim into permanent confinement where he could do no harm to others. At the same time, the victim became available to the "forces of mercy" should these forces decide to rescue the victim, after all, without benefit of the exorcist. Thus, countless people, whose sole problem had been possession, were thrust into dungeons under the supervision of the Inquisition or the Church in general, and expired eventually through neglect.

The popular attitude toward possession combines certain elements of the religious and medical approaches, but adds another dimension—that of fear and superstition. Both physicians and Churchmen knew very well that touching the body of a possessed individual could have no dire consequences for them, since the body belonged to the victim and not to the possessor. But in the popular view, the very touch of the possessed was poisonous and had to be avoided at all costs. Being in the presence of a possessed person or even being looked at by such an individual could have terrible consequences.

Fear, along with total misconception regarding *what* possession was, helped create a false image in the public mind. Ever since the established Church had made it into the work of the devil during the twelfth and thirteenth centuries, the popular version of what happened to the victim included some form of diabolical influence. Whether it was a demon or underling of the devil, or the Great One himself, inevitably there was at work some hellish play that created the dismal state of possession in the victim. It never occurred to the general public that possession could be the result of benevolent interference or anything less than devilish machinations.

In order to understand fully the balanced approach taken by the more progressive of today's parapsychologists (among whom is Professor Hans Holzer), it is necessary to explain briefly what *the Spiritualist approach* to possession is. I have not classed this view among religious approaches, since Spiritualism is not entirely a religious faith but consists of religious elements along with scientifically based conclusions; thus, Spiritualism should occupy a place of its own somewhere between religion and science. In Spiritualism, which is considered a religion by some and an adjunct to their own religions by others, the facts of possession are fully accepted. They are ascribed to the interference of deceased individuals in need of further expression through living bodies and minds. Possession is considered an undesirable situation by Spiritualists, something that has to be dealt with by experienced operators. But the Spiritualist does not exorcise the way a priest does. The Spiritualist *suggests* to the possessing spirit that the spirit's proper place is not within the body and mind of a living human being, but in the world of spirit, which lies just beyond. In suggesting this, the Spiritualist operator then proceeds to request that the possessing spirit mend its ways and go on to the next world. If this is not done, the Spiritualist will cite the dangers that the possessing entity is bringing upon himself by remaining where he clearly does not belong and where he is not wanted. Moralistic principles are involved here and the enticements of the spirit world just beyond the gates are again brought into focus. If all this fails, the Spiritualist will invoke the powers of "spirit," which is a term generally used to refer to the orderly "government" of the spirit world, and with the powers' help will *order* the possessing spirit to depart. In this respect, this is certainly a form of exorcism, although there are none of the physical aspects of it so dear to the Church of the Middle Ages, nor is there any threat of loss of eternal salvation as it is with the Church rite. It is perhaps due to the theory of Spiritualism that the possessing entity is confused in its aims.

Since Spiritualists do not believe in the devil, but treat the possessor as an erring spirit somehow gone astray but worthy of salvation, rather than as a servant of the devil, or the devil himself, as the Church does. The Spiritualist is imbued with his belief in the reality of "summerland," the spirit world, and the orderly way of life in it in which there is essentially only good and no evil; "spirit" controls everything on earth, including people.

The Spiritualistic approach involves clearly uncritical elements of belief and assumption, while at the same time utilizing factual material from the realms of parapsychology as well. Unquestionably, the Spiritualist approach to possession is by far the most useful, short of the psychical research approach, because it is more likely to yield positive results than religious exorcism or purely medical treatment. In defense of religious exorcists and medical practitioners, however, it should be stated that there are individuals among them who are also aware of parapsychology and its findings and who have incorporated some of these findings into their own parochial work. They are just as likely to be successful in their endeavors as the parapsychologist might be.

The reasons for possession may vary greatly according to the individual character of the particular spirits in possession of an individual. They may merely desire to continue physical life through another individual, or it may be due to recognition that some particular individual is especially suited to continue the needs and unfinished business of the deceased individual. In some cases, the living person appeals to the power instinct of the discarnate. Often, the possessor fancies himself or herself in the notion of playing Svengali to some meek Trilby on the earth plane, enjoying the power play as an antidote to the boredom encountered on the spiritual level. This occurs because the discarnate has not yet understood the attractions and possibilities at that level and continues to regard everything from the physical point of view alone.

Eventually the possessing entity familiarizes himself with the thought processes and circumstances of the host personality, for purposes of better control. The more he or she knows about the conditions likely to be encountered inside the body and mind of the host personality, the more the possessor will be able to deal with such conditions. To defend one's hold upon the host personality is foremost in the possessor's mind. To be ejected from the host personality is what the possessor fears and fights at all costs, even sacrificing the life of the host to resist ejection.

Willingness to be possessed is by no means as farfetched as it may sound. To many people, the idea of having a superior will superimposed on their own wills is not only acceptable but desirable. It eliminates the need for their own decisions, shifts the burden of failure from the self to another, and, in general, creates a kind of dependency, which to some is a comfortable refuge from the pressures of the environment. Passive willingness to accept dominance by another is *always* present in cases of possession. In the majority of situations the victim is not even aware of it, but it is nevertheless part of the plot. At the very least, fear of the superior influence of the possessing entity and conviction that nothing can be done about it are present in such cases.

When the willingness or the desire to be possessed turns from passive acceptance to active search and initiation of the relationship, we speak of obsession. As the word indicates, it comes from the Latin *obsedere,* meaning "preoccupied with." The action stems from the victim, not from an outside personality imposed upon the victim. In the broadest sense, obsession means "an abnormal desire with any subject matter" beyond the ordinary.

Professor Hans Holzer tells of one particularly astounding case of possession: "Mary Y. is engaged to be married to a young man of her acquaintance. After a few short weeks the young man is killed in a street accident. Shortly after the funeral, Mary receives spirit communication from the deceased. Thus far, the relationship is entirely within the realm of possibility, as seen by the open-minded psychical researcher. After a while, Mary becomes convinced that she cannot ever forget her dead fiancé nor find another to take his place. To the psychologist this is a simple matter. Mary's mind is becoming unhinged due to excessive grief and her inability to adjust to the environment. But from the parapsychological point of view, something else may be happening. When an occasional communication from the deceased, generally through the mediumship of some local clairvoyant or similar person, is no longer sufficient for Mary and her entire life becomes oriented toward a resumption of the relationship with her dead fiancé, she reaches out to him in the hope of re-establishing a link. At this moment obsession takes place. In Mary's case this obsession may lead to suicide in the hope of joining her loved one on the other side of life. That this is a fallacy can be seen in the light of evidence that suicides rarely reach their goal on the other side of life, but are, to the contrary, sent 'back to school,' as it were, to make up that which they tried to escape on earth.

"Since Mary does not commit suicide and since she cannot be on the same level as her fiancé, she becomes obsessed with him and their further love tie. The continuing relationship develops between two unequal partners, one of the flesh and one in the spirit. As a result of this, Mary shuns all physical relationships on the earth plane, devoting herself entirely to her spirit lover."

On the other hand, there exist cases of sexual possession involving two partners who knew each other before on the earth plane. One partner was cut short by death, either violently or prematurely, and would now seek to continue a pleasurable relationship of the flesh from the new dimension. Deprived of a physical body to express such desires, however, the deceased partner would then find it rather difficult to express the physical desires to the partner remaining on the earth plane. With sex it certainly takes two, and if the remaining partner is not willing, then difficulties will have to be reckoned with. There is the case of Anne C. who "lives with her several children in a comparatively new house in the Northeastern United States. She bought the house eighteen months after her husband had passed away. Thus there was no connection between the late husband and the new house. Nevertheless, her husband's passing was by no means the end of their relationship. 'My husband died five years ago this past September. Ever since then he has not let me have a peaceful day,' she explained in desperation, seeking my help. Two months after her husband had died she saw him coming to her in a dream complaining that she had buried him alive. He explained that he wasn't really dead, and that it was all her fault and all her family's fault that he died in the first place. Mr. C. had lived a rather controversial life, drinking regularly and frequently staying away from home. Thus the relationship between himself and his wife was far from ideal. Nevertheless, there was a strong bond between them. 'In other dreams he would tell me that *he was going to have sex relations with me, whether I wanted him to or not*. He would try to grab me and I

153

would run all through the house with him chasing after me. I never let him get hold of me. He was like that when he was alive, too. The most important thing in life to him was sex and he didn't care how or where he got it. Nothing else mattered to him,' she complained, describing vividly how the supposedly dead husband had apparently still a great deal of life in him. 'He then started climbing on the bed and walking up and down on it and scaring me half to death. I didn't know what it was or what to do about it,' she said, shaking like a leaf."

Popular works, such as *The Exorcist* and *The Devils of Loudoun,* have created the impression that possession by evil individuals is always spectacular, mysterious, and difficult to deal with. This is true only in a minority of cases. There are only so many truly evil individuals capable of gathering within themselves sufficient hatred to perform the necessary operation. The energy required to obtain possession of a flesh-and-blood individual by a discarnate is indeed enormous. That energy reservoir is easier to assemble through hatred than through love, of course. This is so because the desire for evil expression, for hatred, for negative action, is a force unto itself. It can exist in the individual creating it for a long time, before it finds expression through the intermediary of a flesh-and-blood partner. There are many cases where the possessor could not be part of the person's own personality. The evil one possessing the flesh-and-blood person can be identified as a real person who once lived, but of whom the victim knows nothing or had no connection with.

When any would-be exorcist is called upon to help an unfortunate victim of possession, the first thing the exorcist should realize is that he is dealing with *two* individuals—the possessor and the possessed. No matter what has to be done to separate the two, the life and well-being of the possessed individual comes first. In past days this was not always done, and frequently altogether neglected. Since possession is a very real and very serious phenomenon and many past victims have died as a result of overzealous exorcists, every care should be taken to observe the following rules:

Do not use force, especially not physical force, to separate possessed and possessor. Possession is an emotional state and can only be resolved through emotional responses. Electro-shock treatments can do more harm than good. Prior to beginning exorcism, it is important to establish the history of the case. What personality traits have changed over what period of time? When did the seeming possession begin? What was the nature and character of the individual before possession? Such research includes not only family background, economics, religious convictions, and physical condition, but should also include such temporary states as extreme fatigue, nervous tension at a given moment, problems unresolved, hostilities, strong bonds of friendship, and anything else out of the ordinary routine life of the individual that might have been the starting point for the possession relationship.

On the basis of this material, the exorcist can begin to evaluate the case, whether it is one of possession or obsession. Depending upon the feelings and convictions of the victim, he must proceed without offending those convictions. It does little good to warn an atheistic individual of the terrible dangers for his eternal soul when that individual has no use for that soul to begin with. The method of the exorcist must be adapted to each and every circumstance, and there is no hard and fast rule applying to every case.

The exorcist must not permit himself to become party to the case. In other words, emotional involvement on the part of the operator would only be harmful. This is not to be confused with lack of compassion or interest. Just as a doctor should have a warm relationship with his patient and care whether or not he succeeds in healing him, so the exorcist must take a strong and natural interest in the success of his mission. But this must not go beyond the boundaries of an impersonal relationship, no matter how friendly and warm it may be. The use of words is only as practical as the meaning behind them and the emotional tinge given to them when they are pronounced. Even the exorcism of the Church becomes useless when it is intoned without full conviction that it will work. Belief in one's powers and success are an integral and important part of the exorcism. The importance of the ritual cannot be underestimated. Performing certain steps (whether physical movements, intonations of words, or groups of words, or a combination of both, perhaps with the additional emphasis of olfactory stimulants, such as incense, or auditory effects, such as music or drama), has a strong effect upon the bonds existing between the possessor and the possessed. In other words, each and every means at the exorcist's command should be employed, if the means seem likely to loosen those bonds—whether or not such methods can be rationalized or accepted by modern psychology.

In most cases of possession, the possessing entity is more in need of psychiatric care than the possessed. It is the lack of understanding of one's mission in the afterlife that causes possession to take place originally. Therefore, when contact is established with a possessor, whether through the entranced victim or in some other way, it is important to keep in mind that one is dealing with a full personality, even if that personality is demented. Under no circumstances must one pretend that one is really dealing only with a split-off part of the victim's *own* personality and should therefore not humor some nonexisting person; in fact, one is dealing with *two separate individuals*. Any notion that the victim's own characteristics, moral standards, and usual behavior will apply to the actions of the possessor is an illusion—and a dangerous one. By the same token, the victim must in no way be made to feel guilty for being possessed or blamed for the extraordinary actions undertaken by the possessor. Clear distinctions must always be drawn between the two separate individuals.

There is a deep and basic difference between a person experiencing a haunting or communicating with a dead individual and being possessed by someone out of the body, existing in the next dimension. With hauntings, or even with spirit communication, there remains the choice of the communicator either to accept or to reject the communication. Even with the severest hauntings and ghostly visitations (including the physical manifestations known as poltergeist phenomena), there is the choice of leaving the immediate area of the goings-on and moving elsewhere. Ghosts do not follow anyone around. Not so with possessing entities. *The possessed takes his tormentor wherever he travels.* In addition, hauntings and spirit communications indicate merely a desire on the part of the deceased, trapped individual to find a solution to his confusion, or perhaps to communicate his continued existence or to have someone finish unfinished business for him. There is no desire to take over body or mind of anyone for the purpose of continuing an earthly existence. With the possessor, a take-over is the prime motive, and the unfinished business a secondary one.

Fear and hesitation on the part of the exorcist are completely incompatible with the task at hand. Not only would the possessor notice such weaknesses immediately and capitalize on them, but the exorcist himself might be endangering, by exhibiting doubts, the success of his mission. Firm in mind and body, the exorcist must presume to be superior to whatever force he may encounter in the body and mind of the victim.

15
Voodoo

I labored up the dusty hillock by the day's last light. Above me, on the flattened summit, stood a crumbling accretion of cinderblock homes crudely painted white and pale pink. Glassless windows and crumbling facades keynoted the poverty. The stench of human waste and untreated sewage palled the air of the hot summer day on which I was to meet my first hungan, priest, of Voodoo, named Papa Joie. I had come to Port Au Prince to film an episode of the "In Search of . . ." television series dealing with Haiti's mysterious and, for me, at least, frightening religion.

The education I was to receive from Papa Joie would change my view of Voodoo. He demonstrated to me the beauty of its mythology, the strength possessed by its panoply of active spirits, the energy of its fundamental concept. I found that passionate drumbeats, blood, fire, noise and sacrifice coalesce in the Voodoo ceremony in a way that reached deeply into the dark pockets of emotion that I thought modern living had stifled.

My introduction to Voodoo was inauspicious. I arrived at Papa Joie's dampened by the exertion of my climb and dust-laden from the bone-jarring ride to his suburban village in an open cab that Haitians call a "tap-tap." I wasn't quite sure what name to use for the structure in which the Voodoo ceremony was to be held. It was not a church or a temple, nor did it bear a resemblance to any traditional house of religion. A thatched roof crowned raw wooden beams. The walls were stucco over cinderblock. Doorways had no doors; there were no windows per se, just large openings with neither casements nor glass. The floors were dirt. Pathetic little colored streamers hung from strings stretched across the ceiling. The effect was to make the entire place seem

*more run down than it actually was. Papa Joie sat
placidly staring out at the rooftops of plaster shanties
that composed his domain. Around him the hunsai, the
women who were trained in the services of Voodoo, prepared the props for the night's ceremony. All manner
of bottles, specially-cut sticks, palm fronds and an ever-
present rum concoction were being placed in readiness
for the ceremony. Hours later when the last drum had
finished its pulsing song, the last greeting to the spirits
had been sung, I found myself understanding what an
earlier biographer of western Voodoo, Maya Dern, had
written:*

> Possession by the spirits is a reminder that man is of
> divine origin, and heir to an uncounted multitude of
> hearts and minds, that at the root of the universe the
> principles of cosmic good endure, that even under his
> torn shirt, his hunger, the failures of his wit and the
> errors of his heart, his very blood harbors monumental
> spirits.

*Having witnessed the ceremony, I too felt moved and
part of that universal noble spirit.*

More than any other single term, the word *voodoo* is
called to mind whenever mention is made of Haiti. Conceived as a grim system of African practices, it has
come to be identified with fantastic rites and to serve as
a symbol of daring excursions into the esoteric. Its dark
mysteries have been so stressed that it has become customary to think of the Haitians as living in a universe
of psychological terror.

Voodoo, or "Vodun," as it is termed in the native
pronunciation, is a complex of African belief and ritual
governing in large measure the religious life of the
Haitian peasantry.

In Dahomey, the ancient West African kingdom
whence the term has come, Vodun means "God" and is
a general name for all deities. This source of the word
has long been known, I discovered. For example, M. L.
E. Moreau de St.-Mery, in his work *Déscription topo-
graphique, physique, civile, et historique de la partie
française de l'Isle Saint Domingue* (Philadelphia, 1797

and 1798), wrote "According to the Arada Negroes, the real followers of Vaudaux in the colony . . . *Vaudaux* signifies an all-powerful and super-natural being on which depend all the events that come to pass on this globe."

In the New York Public Library I discovered some interesting historical facts. The first is that Vodun derives from a background of African theology and ceremonialism. The second is that Haiti's Blacks have continuously been subjected to a strong influence of Roman Catholicism during the centuries that have passed since their introduction into the island.

Yet another point may prove suggestive in providing a useful point of view for an analysis of the Vodun cult. A fundamental fallacy results from the fact that except where there is an officially sanctioned theology—which makes for dogma, and often for perfunctory worship, in contrast with the living dynamic nature of Haitian peasant belief and ritual—there are no "real" answers to questions in the field of religion. The answers to questions dealing with the same point differ not only according to the status of the individual in the cult, since layman and priest have understandably different concepts of the functions of deities, but also according to the extent of an individual's religious interests.

If the underlying philosophy of the universe held by the Haitians is summarized, this philosophy might be phrased as follows: the ruler of the universe is God, its Creator, who shares this task with His son Jesus, the saints of the Church, and the Holy Ghost. Man has been endowed with a soul, and the soul, which has come from God, returns to God for judgment and, if necessary, for punishment at the end of its sojourn on earth.

From Africa, especially Guinea and Dahomey, the Blacks brought other deities, termed variously *loa, mysteres,* or *saints,* and these deities have been inherited through succeeding generations by the descendants of those who brought them to Haiti. The specific function of the African spirits in the Haitian system was given in the following terms by one of their devotees: "The loa are occupied with men, their task is to cure. They can make a person work better than he otherwise would.

160

When the loa possess people, they give helpful advice. But they cannot do the things that God does. They can protect a garden, but they cannot make a garden grow, for streams, rain, and thunder come from God." Another statement clearly shows the same concept: "God made the loa, but did not make them so they might do evil. When a man purchases a loa for money, that spirit will do evil as well as good, but God becomes angry and will not accept these bad spirits into the sky, and He drives them away."

The most striking element in the Vodun cult is the manner in which the gods are said to "possess" their devotees. Despite the fact that this is the aspect of Haitian religion that seems to the casual observer its least restrained and least disciplined, possession occurs according to well-defined rules and under specifically defined circumstances.

When a person is possessed for the first time, the spirit that is said to animate him is known as a *loa bossal,* an "untamed" god. In the early days the word *bossal* was contemptuously applied to newly arrived Africans. Even today, the same feeling-tone is continued through the belief that since all things in the universe are subject to observable regulation, and animals and plants and human beings must all live according to these rules, the loa, as members of society, may not manifest the unrestrained and often dangerous traits of unpredictable behavior which characterize men before they have been "baptized" and thus brought under proper control.

In native idiom, a person when possessed is "mounted" by his god, and therefore becomes his *ch'wal,* or "horse." A devotee may come under the influence of a number of spirits during a single ceremony or dance, one loa succeeding another. The first deity that ever came to a person, however, for him constitutes the chief of his gods—his *mait'tête*—and the leader of any deities that may subsequently possess him. It is this loa alone that is "baptized" and this one alone "taken from his head" at his death; and, as far as he is concerned, all his other gods are under the control of this *mait'tête,* so that any agreement that he may enter into with this principal spirit must be respected by all others.

In capsule, the Haitian peasant thinks that being possessed by a loa means that an individual's spirit is literally dispossessed by that of the god. Even personalities undergo radical change in accordance with the nature of the deity, and even the sex of the one possessed is disregarded if it differs from that of the god, so that, for example, a woman "mounted" by Ogun is always addressed as Papa Ogun. One wears the colors of the god and the ornaments he likes, eating and drinking those things he prefers, and otherwise manifesting his peculiar characteristics—rolling on the earth, if possessed by Damballa, or chattering incessantly if by Gede.

Worship of the loa is directed by priests of the cult. However, I discovered that the terms *papaloi* and *mamaloi* as designations for male and female priests, almost universally employed by non-Haitian writers, are practically unknown in Haiti, where a priest is called a *hungan,* a priestess a *mambu.*

An important function of the *hungan* or *mambu* is to foretell the future, and it is as a diviner that the Vodun priest or priestess is most often employed. No major rite would be considered by a family unless divination was resorted to, but consultation is made for a far wider range of affairs than those of a purely religious nature. No proposed undertaking of any importance is begun without visiting a diviner. When divining, the priest is usually under possession by his gods, but other methods, such as gazing into a crystal ball or basin of water, may also be employed. In reading about Haiti, I found that a weird, diabolical legend has been created around the Vodun religion. Writers portrayed Haiti as a magic island bursting with phantoms, zombies, and devils; and their themes obscured the true spirit of Vodun.

This was the situation until the science of ethnography took a hand in the question: as facts fell into place, and found their rightful meaning, it was realized that there was a strong, distinctive culture; and with this realization came an effort to recover the essence of this culture. The ethnographers, however, encountered an additional obstruction: a contemporary school of writers sympathetic to Vodun interpret it in the light of Kabalism.

The origin of this particular trend lies in those ancient Vodun principles which, if examined perfunctorily, might well be confused with some of the Gnostic traditions. For Vodun is a religion of mysteries and of initiatic character; one of its manifestations is a fervor-impelled ecstasy, the loa crisis, in which the worshiper attains a state of ultimate exaltation. There is, basically, nothing mystical about this crisis that takes place within the framework of the Vodun religion and is achieved through suggestion, or auto-suggestion. Only during the "hunsi-canzo" initiation rites, which are based on purely spiritual meditation, the crisis is the result of genuine mysticism, arising from the teachings that foreshadow and suggest it.

The origins of this initiation, symbolizing the fall of the soul into the evil world of darkness and its efforts to disentangle itself from evil matter so as to return to the upper world of light, with the intervention of intermediary spirits (angels of darkness resembling the Legions of Catholicism), are indeed to be found in antiquity.

Interestingly enough, numerous aspects of the Vodun show clearly that this religion accepts the concept of the Christian Word: the names of Jesus and Mary are venerated in all ceremonies; Christian prayers mingle with African invocations, and although he heads the Vodun pantheon, Shango, the African god, has given way to Christ. The intermediary spirits, or loa, have been assimilated to Catholic saints; in the hunfort temples, the enthroned crucifixes as well as the imagery are Roman Catholic. There are no ceremonies that do not include both Christ and Papa Legba.

A major factor is Vodun's acceptance of the Roman calendar; this enabled the former slaves to keep pace with the living routines of their colonial masters. Today, Roman Catholic saint's days and loa celebration dates overlap one another. In Haiti's major religious ceremonies, which attract participants from every part of the land, it is interesting to observe the interlacement of

African practices with the rites of French liturgical folklore; despite the clergy's attempts to discourage these practices, Haitians insist on giving the Vodun side its due.

Vodun ceremonies in today's Haiti have two distinct forms, the Rada and the Pétro. The Rada ceremonies are the older of the two, with their origins in Africa itself. They are dedicated to deities that are said to shun violence. Pétro rites, on the other hand, were born in the New World. They are Haitian in origin, and addressed to deities that represent the forces of violence. Just as the protective Rada deities have grown out of the generally stable society of the West African kingdom of Dahomey, so the aggressive Pétro deities made their appearance in direct reaction to the brutalities of the slave system, responding to the Blacks' need to strike back against the exploitation.

In Pétro ceremonies, two instruments unknown to the Rada ritual are used: the whip and the whistle. The crack of the whip calls the Pétro "spirits," concentrating and releasing the power of the active and violent loa. The shrill sound of the whistle serves to dramatize the ceremonies. In the Vodun temple, the whip is tied to the wall or to the central pole, the *poteau legba,* which supports the apex of the thatched pavilion. This incongruous instrument in a sacred place of worship is always impressive and moving.

Like the cross and the sword, which also have their places in the temple, the whip is a symbol that has more than one meaning. For example, the sword, whose blade is thrust into the ground in front of the altar of the hunfort, is part of a traditional African ritual to halt the spirits. It is also a reminder to the modern Haitian that his freedom was prepared in secret Vodun meetings, and that he had to conquer his masters to win his liberty. The cross, Vodun symbol of the crossroads and of contact with the four corners of the world, is inherited from ancient African rituals. Its presence reminds the Haitian peasant of the cross of Christ that he sees in church, as well as in the village hunfort.

The educated classes in Haiti—mulattoes brought up in the French tradition and sometimes educated in

France—comprise only about ten percent of the total population. A people of black peasants, who live in huts of mud and lath, practice the Voodoo religion, which the Blacks brought with them from Africa, and speak Creole, a rudimentary language compounded of African and French.

The cultivated people of Haiti were ashamed of this primitive race, and the writers as a rule ignored it. But in 1928, a Haitian scientist, Dr. Jean Price-Mars, published a book called *Ainsi Parla l'Oncle: Essais d'Ethnographie,* which proved to be a literary landmark. Dr. Price-Mars urged upon Haitians the importance of coming to terms with the culture of the Black lower classes, pointing out that their superstitions played a much more considerable role in the psychology of the educated people than they were generally willing to admit, and made a plea for the native writers to address themselves to the presentation of Haitian life in all its aspects.

I have witnessed the petro, the blood and fire of the dark Voodoo ritual. My tradition and heritage are vastly different from that of the people who bank their lives on the outcome of the ceremony. Yet as I examine the world of magic and witchcraft, I will never be a naysayer to its effects, for by the dawn's early light on a Haitian hilltop I felt the flush of primitive passion that for all time has made me say, "I believe."

BIBLIOGRAPHY

Ahmed, Rollo. *The Black Art*. Arrow, 1966.

Anonymous. "The Whistle and the Whip," *Tomorrow* magazine, 1954.

Cohen, Daniel, *Curses, Hexes and Spells*. Philadelphia: Lippincott, 1974.

Conway, David. *Magic*. New York: E. P. Dutton, 1972.

Cunningham, Sara. Stonehenge (list), 1975.

Gardner, Gerald. *The Meaning of Witchcraft*. New York: Samuel Weiser, 1971.

Gatti, Arthur. *The Kennedy Curse*. Chicago: Henry Regnery, 1976.

de Givry, Emile Grillot. *A Pictorial Anthology of Witchcraft, Magic and Alchemy*. New York: University Books, 1958.

Herskovits, Melville J. "What is Vodoo?" *Tomorrow* magazine, 1954.

Holzer, Hans. *Possessed/An Exorcist's Casebook*. New York: Fawcett, 1973.

————. *The Alchemist*. Briarcliff Manor, N.Y.: Stein & Day, 1973.

————. *The Habsburg Curse*. New York: Doubleday, 1973.

————. *The Human Dynamo*. Milbrae, Calif.: Celestial Arts, 1975.

————. *The New Pagans*. New York: Doubleday, 1972.

————. *The Truth About Witchcraft*. New York: Doubleday, 1969.

————. *The Witchcraft Report*. New York: Ace, 1973.

Huson, Paul. *Mastering Herbalism*. Briarcliff Manor, N.Y.: 1974.

————. *Mastering Witchcraft*. New York: Putnam, 1970.

Marple, Eric. *Witchcraft*. Octopus Books, 1973.

Maximilien, Louis. "Voodoo, Gnosis, Catholicism," *Tomorrow* magazine, 1954.

O. T. A. *The Seventh Day*, (pamphlet), 1975.

Scholem, Gershom G. *On the Kabbalah and Its Symbolism*. New York: Schocken, 1965.

Smyth, F. *Modern Witchcraft*. Macdonald, 1970.

St. Farrar. *What Witches Do*. New York: Coward-McCann & Geoghegan, 1971.

Wilson, Edmund. "Voodoo in Literature," *Tomorrow* magazine, 1954.